Middle Eastern Lives

Contemporary Issues in the Middle East

Published in cooperation with
the Moshe Dayan Center for
Middle Eastern and African Studies
Tel Aviv University

Middle Eastern Lives

The Practice of Biography and Self-Narrative

Edited by Martin Kramer

Syracuse University Press

First Edition 1991
91 92 93 94 95 96 97 98 99   6 5 4 3 2 1

The paper used in this publication meets the minimum
requirements of American National Standard for
Information Sciences—Permanence of Paper for Printed
Library Materials, ANSI Z39.48-1984. ∞™

LIBRARY OF CONGRESS CATALOGING-IN-
PUBLICATION DATA

Middle Eastern lives : the practice of biography and self-
    narrative / edited by Martin Kramer. — 1st ed.
        p.   cm. — (Contemporary issues in the Middle East)
    Proceedings of a conference sponsored by the Moshe
Dayan Center for Middle Eastern and African Studies.
    "Published in cooperation with the Moshe Dayan
Center for Middle Eastern and African Studies. Tel Aviv
University."
    Includes bibliographical references and index.
    ISBN 0-815602548-0 (alk. paper)
    1. Biography (as a literary form)—Congresses.
2. Autobiography—Authorship—Congresses.
3. Middle East—Biography—History and criticism—
Congresses.   4. Self in literature—Congresses.
I. Kramer, Martin S. II. Merkaz Dayan le-ḥeḳer ha-
Mizraḥ ha-tikhon ve-Afriḳah (Universiṭat Tel-Aviv)
III. Series.
CT21.M54   1991
808'.06692—dc20   91-11277

Manufactured in the United States of America

Contents

Preface   vii

Introduction   1
Martin Kramer

1. First-Person Narrative in the
    Middle East   20
    Bernard Lewis

2. Traditional Islamic Learning and Ideas
    of the Person in the Twentieth Century   35
    Dale F. Eickelman

3. Autobiography and Biography
    in the Middle East: A Plea for
    Psychopolitical Studies   60
    Marvin Zonis

4. Biography and Psychohistory   89
    Elie Kedourie

5. A Response to Critics of a
    Psychobiography   97
    Vamik D. Volkan and Norman Itzkowitz

6.   History versus Biography   109
     Shabtai Teveth

7.   The Biographical Element in
     Political History   118
     Uriel Dann

8.   A Sampler of Biography and
     Self-Narrative   127
     Martin Kramer

     Notes   147
     Contributors   159
     Index   161

Preface

The last few years have seen an upsurge of interest in biography and autobiography across a wide range of disciplines. The appeal of both, as genre and source material, is owed to a new appreciation for narrative, but even more to the quest for a shared humanism. As academic specialties narrow, the practice of biography and the interpretation of self-narrative constitute common ground, where scholars can conduct a dialogue in which no discipline enjoys a uniquely privileged position.

This volume contains the proceedings of a small gathering meant to open that dialogue. These are papers presented at a conference convened at Tel Aviv University in 1987. The participants, although few in number, included scholars from the disciplines of anthropology, history, political science, and psychology. Some spoke as writers of biographies; others, as critics of biographies and self-narratives. Some presented research papers; others, essays of opinion. The objective was not to cover the Middle East geographically (although the articles do draw on Turkish, Iranian, Arab, and Israeli examples). Rather, the aim was to explore alternative approaches to evidence. The contributors avoided the rarefied theoretical issues that have preoccupied postmodernist critics of literary biography. Their concerns were more practical. How does one persuasively write a life? How does one persuasively use self-narrative as evidence? The wide diversity of approaches produced much heat and also some light, and a sense of shared enterprise that I hope this book conveys.

I wish to thank a number of persons and institutions for their support for the conference and this publication. I am especially grateful to Prof. Itamar Rabinovich, then Director of the Moshe Dayan Center for Middle Eastern and African Studies at Tel Aviv University, who assisted at every stage in the preparation of the conference, and to my colleague on the organizing committee, Prof. Saul Friedländer of Tel Aviv University. The conference and book were made possible thanks to the Moshe Dayan Center for Middle Eastern and African Studies at Tel Aviv University, which sponsored the conference; the Conference Board of Tel Aviv University, which covered some of the expenses; the America-Israel Educational Foundation (Fulbright Commission), which contributed to participants' travel; and the Lucius N. Littauer Foundation, which made a grant toward publication of the book. At the Dayan Center, Mrs. Lydia Gareh typed the manuscript with her customary exactitude, and Mrs. Edna Liftman steered the book safely through bureaucratic shoals. I wish to extend a special word of gratitude to Ms. Cynthia Maude-Gembler of Syracuse University Press for taking the volume under her benevolent wing and seeing it to publication.

It is my hope that this slim volume will initiate a broader discussion of how our understanding of the Middle East might be enriched by the study of individual lives.

Chicago, Illinois   MARTIN KRAMER
January 1991

Middle Eastern Lives

Introduction

Martin Kramer

THE Middle East and the West are heirs to long traditions of recounting lives. In the ancient civilizations of the Mediterranean and west Asia, the stories of individuals were chiseled on friezes and triumphal arches, minted on coins, memorized as epic, and written down as chronicle. Although Christendom and Islam arose to proclaim the unlimited power of a single God, they made still more generous allowance for the role of the exemplary life in divine history. Both traditions rested upon individual responsibility before an indivisible God, who worked his will through the lives of prophets and kings, saints and warriors. Christians and Muslims differed over the precise manifestation of the divine presence, but they differed not at all in their search for guidance in the edifying lives of Jesus and Muhammad, the disciples and the companions, St. Augustine and Ghazali, Richard the Lionhearted and Saladin. Within both great traditions, the recording of lives became a specialization within the preservation of knowledge, and the recorders followed similar conventions of selection and narration. And in both traditions, the purpose of organizing the circumstances of a life was overwhelmingly didactic, to inspire and guide by example.

It was the West that discovered a new and revolutionary way of telling lives, at a time when, for many of the same reasons, the West was discovering much else that was new and revolutionary. What would become modern biography and autobiography differed from the old telling in their insistence on the intellectual and emotional distance of the teller from the subject—even when that subject was the self. These modern biographers sought evidence of human motive where their predecessors cited divine intervention. In the quest for knowing, they sought to penetrate those corners of lives left unexplored by the traditional edifiers and hagiographers.

This distancing ultimately made biography one of the grandest spires of nineteenth- and early-twentieth-century historiography and established introspective autobiography as a major form of literary expression. In the past hundred years, recorded lives achieved a cultural ideal in form and proportion, an ideal preserved to this day in many biographies and autobiographies. Narrative proceeds in some chronological relationship to the lived life. It draws on the public document and the private diary to weave a coherent story, in which the subject always occupies center stage. Bolder narratives, influenced primarily by psychoanalysis and the modern novel, seek to reconstruct perception and hidden motive, of others and the self. And the narrative champions fullness as the highest virtue, so that a biography, to approach truth, must be comprehensive. Its proportions must evoke the creative (or destructive) energy generated by a lived life.

But this revolution in the telling of lives did not sweep the Muslim societies of the Middle East. Muslims immediately associated intellectual distance with disbelief, for they were introduced to the methods of modern biography largely by Orientalists, who applied them to the edifying lives of the Islamic tradition, and especially the life of the Prophet Muhammad.[1] In the nineteenth century, Muslim opinion became much exercised over the subjection of Muhammad's life and other exemplary Muslim lives to the critical methods of Western biographers. Some in the Middle East, battered by the political and cultural expansion of the West, rejected the desacralization of their history, as they have done in our own time by their condemnation of Salman Rushdie's *The Satanic Verses*. To make sacred lives the subject of critical biography was to commit a sacrilege. The situation did not differ much among those who substituted the creed of nationalism for the religion of Islam. Nationalism, too, edified through the telling of exemplary lives and created its own personality cults. And so the writing of Middle Eastern lives in the Middle East largely followed the methodological and intellectual ground rules of traditional and uncritical narration. The same held true for self-narration, which was either devoid of introspection or more like memoir than autobiography.

Orientalism and "New" History

The first initiatives in applying critical methods to Middle Eastern lives originated largely from outside the region. Even these were slow in coming, for a subtle bias against biography ran through the Orientalist tradition. Whereas the "old" historian of Europe respected and even exalted the causal role of the individual, the Orientalist insisted on the primacy of culture as expressed in language and religion. Compelling history was not the doings of rulers and their dynasties, although Orientalists did much to establish the chronology of Islamic history and to translate chronicles. Compelling history was cultural history—the history of religion, philosophy, and literature—

which evidenced change over time, often through the influences of other cultures. Orientalists therefore produced a very limited corpus of biography. Studies of towering figures were compiled, including the biographies of the Prophet that Muslims found offensive, but the Orientalist history of Islam was largely the history of a religious community, in which the individual was rarely accorded the full autonomy attributed to the individual Westerner.

Nor did the Orientalists receive encouragement from the example of the "new" history as it emerged early in this century. The "new" historians of Europe had little use for biography once they had shifted the territory of historical inquiry from elite to mass, from politics to society. Vast segments of society had been excluded from the "old" history, even of Europe. The "new" historian sought evidence for the driving forces of change in villages and town marketplaces, not in courts and palaces. Change itself originated not in the action or inaction of rulers or a ruling elite but in economic, demographic, and ecological forces that unfolded over long durations of time. These constituted the fundamental tiers on which human history rested—so deep and vast that only a total vision of history could encompass them in its sweep. The biography of the "great man" in the nineteenth-century tradition did not disappear, but it was undertaken increasingly by nonprofessional historians who wrote for general audiences. Academic historians questioned not only the utility of biography but its very legitimacy.

When historiography's European revolution occurred, it led the historiography of the Middle East almost directly from Orientalism to "new" history. The transformation was swiftest in France. There the domineering figure of Louis Massignon personified the metamorphosis of Orientalist into social and economic historian. Under the proximate influence of the *Annalistes,* he and other scholars, who had been formed in the tradition of Oriental studies, rushed straight into social and economic history. Maxime Rodinson, trained in philology, followed a similar progression to economic history, although under the rather different impetus of Marxist theory. French scholarship passed through no stage comparable to the "old" history, with its emphasis on politics and biography, but leapt, like Massignon and Rodinson, directly from philology and religion to the study of guilds and prices. When they paused to study individual lives—Massignon that of Hallaj, Rodinson that of Muhammad—their quest was not for the unique but for the exemplary and edifying, although their criteria differed radically from those of Muslims.

In the English-speaking world, the transformation of Orientalist into "new" historian was not as dramatic. Yet the same leap was urged by the Orientalist Sir Hamilton Gibb, who argued that the next generation should devote its resources to social history. "It is vital to stress the word 'society,'" he wrote three decades ago, for "the nature and pressures of the internal social forces engaged have largely determined the working of [Middle Eastern] political structures."[2] The admonition did not go unheeded. In a comprehensive survey of Middle Eastern historiography published slightly more than a decade ago, the historian Albert Hourani announced that "social history seems likely to be the dominant mode of history writing for the present generation."[3] That generation borrowed theoretical models and methodologies first elaborated by the "new" historians of Europe, who had defined the concerns of social history when most Middle Eastern history still was being written by Orientalists. In recent years historians of the Middle East have produced the first studies to employ the paradigms of political economy, the "world-system," the *Annales* approach, and even deconstructionism. In the words of one "new" historian of the Middle East, the search is for a paradigm that "is able to describe the activities of the whole society as meaningful, and need not restrict itself to a narrative of political events and elite biography, disembodied from the rest of society."[4] Nothing in the work of the Orientalists ever quite approximated this avid depersonalization of Muslim society.

"It has been said that when ideas die in France, they are reborn in America," one eminent American historian has written. "One might add that when they are past their prime in other disciplines, they are belatedly adopted by historians."[5] And only after they have made their contributions to the history of Europe are they applied to the history of the Middle East. By the time the first "new" historians of the Middle East emerged, the general crisis of the "new" history—what one practitioner once called "history without people"—had already overtaken the field. The crisis grew from a disappointment with the yield of "total history" and doubts about the role of such history as a humanistic endeavor. Over the past decade, narrative history has been revived, and even biography has lost much of its stigma.

The crisis of the "new" history is just now being appreciated by historians of the Middle East. Their disillusionment is bound to be deeper, for in every instance the resort to the themes and methods of the "new" history has been less satisfactory for the Middle East than for Europe. The thinness of the sources and the complete absence of many social groups from the extant records has left the "new" history of the Middle East a pale shadow of its European models. The "thick description" that several historians have achieved for parts of premodern Europe can never be approximated for the Middle East. And so historians of the Middle East are becoming aware of the revaluation of biography as evidenced in the work of historians of Europe, the creation of new journals of biographical method, and the choice of biography as a theme of conferences held by advanced research institutes. There are signs of a new willingness among historians of the Middle East to see whether biography can produce a fuller and richer representation of the past. And there is a readiness to look again at self-narratives, in order to mine new insights from the texts.

Obstacles to Representation

Yet this new endeavor cannot but bring into relief the special problems of writing Middle Eastern lives, for it may be just as difficult to follow the lead of "new" biography on Middle Eastern ground as it was to follow the lead of "new" history.

The "new" biographer, like the "new" historian, cannot discount the dearth of intimate source materials. There are no comprehensive and accessible collections of private papers, no confidential diaries deposited for the scrutiny of all. Certainly there have always been sufficient sources for those seeking to write about one or another Middle Eastern writer, and many of those schooled in the strong Orientalist traditions of cultural and literary history contributed to what might be called intellectual biography or portraiture. Yet this writing was often disembodied, based narrowly on the works of the subjects themselves. There were too few intimate documents to surround public text with context. That there can be a wide discrepancy between the public and private persona of a Muslim intellectual we know from the successive lives of Sayyid Jamal al-Din "al-Afghani," reckoned as the precursor of the major Muslim ideological responses to the modern West. With each chance discovery of material—a file in the British Public Records Office, another in the French police archives, and finally some of his own papers in a Tehran library—it became clear how futile trying to assess Afghani's life solely through his own writings had been. No one can say how many lives of Muslim intellectuals might be turned over by the discovery of a trunk of letters. But these lives were not lived in Bloomsbury. Cairo, Damascus, Istanbul, Tehran—these cities insisted on conformity, in politics, literature, and art. An intellectual might dare to stretch these conventions but could never openly defy them. And so it is almost impossible to strip away the heavy layers of self-imposed censorship; in many instances, the absence of letters and diaries means that the private voice is forever lost.

The intimate sources for the lives of rulers and leaders remain even more inaccessible. There is nothing Middle Eastern about the desire of the powerful to erect defensive barriers between their personas and themselves, but the powerful of the Middle East sometimes have erected barriers so high as to be insurmountable, even decades later. "Political biography is essentially concerned with the interaction of personality and politics," one historian has written. "And personality, it is commonly supposed, is at least as much the product of private as of public experiences. How then are political biographies of

Middle Eastern leaders possible? For their private lives are as secluded from public gaze as were the family lives of their fathers, secure behind the windowless outer walls of their dwellings. Syrian presidents disclose what they choose: in place of personalities they have personality cults."[6] Even when those cults die—usually superseded by the cult of a successor—the evidence for the lived life remains fragmentary or inaccessible.

As a consequence, some modern lives that occupied the center of history's canvas have never been told with documentary rigor. No documented biographies present the lives of Ottoman sultan Abdülhamid II and Qajar shah Nasir al-Din, the two rulers who dominated the Islamic world in which Afghani lived, and who reigned for thirty-three and forty-eight years, respectively. (A scholarly biography of Nasir al-Din is now in preparation.) There is no life of Faysal, the leader of the Arab revolt, ruler in Damascus, and then king in Baghdad. There are a number of biographies of their successors—of Egyptian and Syrian and Turkish presidents, of Iranian shahs and Arabian kings. But these works, when they are not journalistic, have been forced to rely on secondary sources because the intimate document is inaccessible. Sometimes interviews can offer compensation, but the intimate document is biography's adrenaline. If we know Herzl better than Abdülhamid II, Lawrence better than Faysal, Philby better than Ibn Saud, Eden better than Nasser, it is largely thanks to the rich texture of the sources. There is no substitute.

Or is there? All lives leave their documentary gaps; perhaps the documentary problem for the Middle East is one of degree rather than kind. Just as there cannot be total history, there cannot be total biography. All biography, like all history, is a grand compromise. One biographical strategy is to narrow the focus to questions suggested by the accessible evidence. This is the essence of "political biography," a life told with an explicit bias for politics and the kinds of available evidence that politics generates. Another strategy is to draw on some theory to infer a world of meaning from the broadest circumstances and anecdotal details of a life. This is the essence of "psychobiography," a life told through explicit inferences, guided by a more or less comprehensive theory of motive. Both of these approaches to biography are compromises: the first because of its willful omissions, the second because of its deliberate inferential leaps.

A great deal has been written and said about the problems raised by such compromises. Here it need only be noted that they are often greater for the biographer of a Middle Eastern subject. The political biographer may not have access to the private diary, but if the life of a subject was lived within the confines of a Western democracy, the public archives are probably copious and accessible. Yet in much of the Middle East and during most periods, politics have been conducted much like private life—behind high walls of secrecy, secure from all scrutiny. In what sense is the president of Syria, even after twenty years of rule, a "public man"? Is it not more accurate to say that he is Syria's most private man, whereas it is the citizens of Syria who are public men and women, who live their lives under the penetrating gaze reserved in the West for the politicians? The political biographer of the Middle Eastern leader is compelled to make not a few leaps of faith in trying to reconstruct the concealed dynamics of decisions for which the evidence is fragmentary at best.

In one sense, the compromise demanded of the psychobiographer of a Middle Eastern subject is no greater than that demanded of any psychobiographer. For adherents of comprehensive theories, the inferential leaps built into theory are essentially the same regardless of cultural setting. Yet in practice, those leaps may be longer and more perilous for the psychobiographer of a Middle Eastern subject. At many times and in many places, the experience of private, family, and sexual life in the Middle East has differed radically from the kinds of experience that have driven theory in the West. And since so little has been done even to describe the range of experience in the Middle East, from palace life to tent life, it is difficult to determine just where the biases might lie. The distance of the leap is further lengthened by a certain sense of propriety and privacy common to most of the Middle East. This transforms self-revelation into a breach of collective integrity, makes women invisible, and constricts the flow of evidence.

But if the Middle Eastern setting of biography raises the obstacles, it also raises the incentives. For in the Middle East, almost as much as in Europe, this has been a century of "great men." The Middle East entered the century under the traditional authority of long-ruling sultans and shahs. After an imperial interlude, the charismatic authority of revolutionary heroes had its moment of (vain)glory. A decline in the apparent caliber of leaders occurred just after midcentury, when the Middle East became a cauldron of coups. Historians and social scientists had little cause to dwell on the many rulers who shuttled in and out of office during those years. The prize of these incessant struggles could scarcely be called power, since a growing dependence narrowed the base of resources—social, economic, military—that could support leader-driven change. But in the last two decades, new wealth has combined with new technologies of control to transform some Middle Eastern leaders into immovable strongmen.

With the collapse of the despotisms of Eastern Europe, the Middle East remains the last preserve of protracted individual rule. Syria's president has ruled for twenty years. Jordan's king has reigned for thirty-seven years. Libya's leader brought off his coup twenty years ago. The chairman of the Palestine Liberation Organization has held his title for twenty years. Iraq's ruler helped to bring his party to power twenty years ago, and has ruled the country alone for ten years. Now that the means of control have been supplemented by the technologies of mass destruction, the "great men" loom large. Through cults of personality that they themselves promote, they have become the embodiments of entire states. Their enhanced stature, of course, is partly an illusion, a game of mirrors. The revolutions of Eastern Europe hang over the "great men" of the Middle East like a pall. But the recent history of some Middle Eastern polities is virtually inseparable from the choices and prejudices of a few men. For periods when strong leaders rule, as in Europe during the age of the dictators and in the Middle East today, biography becomes indispensable to history. And so it must be, unless or until Middle Eastern societies rise up to impose some limitation on ambition and personal power.

Competing Approaches

Reading and writing lives begin with careful listening to the voices of those who have lived them. Self-narrative in its various forms is the subject of the first two essays in this volume, by

Bernard Lewis and Dale Eickelman, and of much of the third, by Marvin Zonis. Lewis considers the nature of the self-narratives that have figured in the literatures of the Middle East from ancient times to the present, with an emphasis on the Islamic tradition. His point is to demonstrate the continuous thread of self-narrative in these literatures and thus refute the argument that only under Western impact have Middle Easterners given accounts of their own lives. It is a point well taken: the past offers up numerous apologia, self-aggrandizing statements to posterity, and first-person accounts of religious awakening. Yet as Lewis points out, much of this material is of a fragmentary nature and contains little that might be described as introspective.

A question Lewis does not raise, but one that is inescapable, is whether this paucity of introspection is the product of culture. In his essay, Marvin Zonis goes further: noting the dearth of true autobiography in the Middle East, he argues that the retrospective assignment of meaning to a life, so essential to the production of introspective autobiography, is a product of Western historicism. Life experience is not integrated or understood as a variable fashioned by changing contexts; the lived life is understood as a series of discrete experiences. The predominant cultures of the Middle East, with their emphasis on communal values and identity, do not encourage an individualism essential to introspection. These cultural norms preclude more than true autobiography, since true biography also depends on the same sense of historicism and individualism. As Dale Eickelman suggests in his essay, this devaluation of individual will owes nothing to Islam and indeed would seem to stand in opposition to Islamic doctrine, which stresses personal responsibility and autonomy. But that doctrine has always been in tension with social values inherited from pre-Islam.

On all these points, Zonis enters controversial ground. The postulated inability to integrate a life's experience cannot but evoke those formulations about the atomism of Arab thought so attacked by the critics of Orientalism. The argument that communalism undervalues liberty and equality, and that the Middle Easterner understands only fraternity, has been made before. Yet the fact remains that very little self-narrative by Middle Easterners satisfies the criteria by which Westerners define true autobiography. If Middle Eastern self-narrative is thin, its thinness requires methodological strategies to compensate for the lacunae.

As Dale Eickelman demonstrates, the anthropologist can supplement the self-narrative by firsthand observation of the wider social context. Eickelman has studied the *tarjama,* highly stylized self-narrative or biography, of learned men in local settings in both Morocco and Oman. These texts show some evolution in form but remain almost rigidly stylized and selective, offering nothing in the way of introspection or accounting of motive. The texts serve above all to present the cultural personas of learned men: their social masks, put on for the benefit of a contemporary audience of initiates. The tarjamas exclude family context, peer learning, economic activity, and politics— precisely the subject matter sought by the anthropologist in the quest for contextual wholeness. As it happens, the tarjamas consulted by Eickelman are ambiguous about just those political issues that most interest him: the relationship of individual men of learning to French colonial rule in Morocco, and their attitude to the imamate in Oman. Such texts then are not self-contained, but once their context is established through direct observation, they become invaluable documents, not only for what they include, but just as often for what they omit. The marked discrepancies between what the tarjamas say about these learned men and what Eickelman has found out about them can only sober the historical biographer, who must rely solely on texts and recollections to reconstruct lives.

Eickelman's kind of "social biography" is not so much the reading of lives as it is reading between the lines of lives. And for some, it is not particular context but universal theory that coaxes the alternative readings from the texts. The second part of the essay by Marvin Zonis advocates the resort to psychological theory to illuminate what he calls the human "black box." His plea for psychopolitical studies is not precisely a plea for psychobiography: the psychopolitical study is in every instance the case study of an event, not a life, and depends just as much on group psychology. Yet certainly in the case chosen by Zonis, the fall of Iran's last shah, an abbreviated psychobiography is the inevitable prelude to the study itself.

Ultimately, then, any plea for psychopolitical studies is a plea for psychobiography. In the case of the Shah's fall, Zonis seeks to demonstrate how much can be added to an understanding of Iran's revolution by accounting for the Shah's own conduct—and how much more convincingly that conduct can be explained through psychoanalytic theory. Drawing particularly on the work of Heinz Kohut, Zonis maintains that "the Shah entered adult status with depleted narcissism, unable to provide himself with a level of self-esteem sufficient to allow the maintenance of a reasonable psychic equilibrium. Instead, he was totally dependent for his narcissistic nurturing on external sources." As it happened, each of those sources failed him as the revolution gathered steam, leaving him quite helpless to resist it. When personality becomes the pivot of explanation, so too does a theory of personality.

The difficulty, of course, is that theories of personality stir deep disagreements among theorists and evoke charges of determinism and reductionism among historians. Zonis argues for tolerance and a kind of suspension of judgment, but the warriors of theory take no prisoners. Vamik D. Volkan and Norman Itzkowitz, whose psychoanalytic biography *The Immortal Atatürk* evoked many hostile reactions, respond in kind to their critics. The assumption of their piece is that the "unending" argument over the validity of psychoanalysis cannot be resolved: "Let them have it how they will." More consequential for them are the objections of psychoanalysts to psychoanalytic biography, criticism made within the charmed circle of believers. For psychoanalysis is both a theory and a clinical technique that "brings the analyst and analysand together in a highly specific way." This interaction between analyst and analysand generates the very evidence on which the entire analysis rests. Not surprisingly, many psychoanalysts are uncomfortable with the application of their techniques of interpretation to dead, unanalyzed subjects. Volkan and Itzkowitz respond by showing how texts and interviews related to Atatürk can supply some of the information that would have been gained from an actual analysis of the Turkish leader. This information can interact usefully with theory, although they concede that "total biography" is impossible.

For Elie Kedourie, however, this attempt by psychobiographers (and others) to hang their evidence on a shaky scaffold of theory—and then deduce what is hidden and missing—is self-delusion. Biography, like any historical account, "is wholly made up of pieces of evidence interlocking with other similar pieces without, so to speak, being forced. And if there is no evidence, then no concept can make up for its absence." For Kedourie, "there is nothing beyond or above or below the historical record (as the evidence shows it to be) which may serve to account for or to explain this record." The record is "its own explanation." Nor do the biographer and the subject need the mediation of theoretical decoding: mind is akin to mind, mind speaks to mind, mind can and does understand mind.

Kedourie's repudiation of the social sciences is a view that has few adherents among historians outside Britain. During the conference, the historian Saul Friedländer, who served as commentator, proposed the compromise of "limited models." But there would seem to be little middle ground on which a Kedourie and a Volkan or Itzkowitz might meet. Practically speaking, the debate over psychobiography has probably gone as far as it can go. Nothing done on the Middle East is likely to carry it much further.

The last two essays, one by a biographer, the other by a political historian, consider the relationship of biography to history. Compared to biographers of most Middle Eastern subjects, biographer Shabtai Teveth works in a very different medium, for writing the lives of the makers of Israel rests on introspective sources that are plentiful and accessible. Yet even here Teveth finds history and biography at odds. First, whereas history proclaims the primacy of evidence, biography is an art; it insists on a "blend of evidence and poetic licence." (Some contributors to this volume invoke theories of science to sanction inferential leaps; others claim the licenses of art—both for the same purpose.) Second, history and biography diverge in assignations of significance. The choice of biography is itself a selection, even an exclusion, that blue-pencils a question mark beside every digression of narrative into the wider context of events. Yet for biography to do credible service as history, it must draw the full-length portrait of its subject's life and the context of that life. (This may explain why biographies often run to such great length.) But if biography is indeed a "crime against history," as Teveth says, then it is certainly no more heinous than the offenses committed daily in the name of new theories and methods. Certainly Teveth's own study of Ben-Gurion qualifies as history, for the lived life is tightly interwoven with the dramatic events of the time. Yet biography's demands of style, proportion, and emphasis will doubtless continue to repel some historians, even as they attract ever-growing numbers of readers.

Uriel Dann contemplates the other side of the coin. Just how much biography can be usefully introduced into a political history? Quite a bit, Dann concludes, especially in the setting of the Middle East, where the "prevalence of a hero" makes insistent biographical demands on the political historian. Dann himself has always accepted the challenge; each of his political histories has turned on the axis of a central figure. Just how much biography is essential and how much is intrusive in political history is a matter of—well, plain common sense: "There is no ironclad definition of what is 'palpably trivial,' but we are expected, after all, to exercise some judgment." Theories and models notwithstanding, there is no substitute for sound judgment, a capacity for empathy, and a strong respect for evidence. This is not historical fundamentalism, but simply a reminder that all interpretation must rest on firm foundations.

The Promise of Biography

In a book full of pleas and admonitions, a general one in favor of the book's theme is not out of order. When done with sensitivity, the telling and reading of lives increase our empathy for people of other times, other places, other cultures. There are many other roads to other minds (history, language, literature), but few so resistant to the arid pedantry of over-specialization as biography. Biography allows scholars in warring disciplines to debate their differences on the neutral ground of a shared humanism, where no discipline enjoys a uniquely privileged position. And biography and autobiography are literary forms that are appreciated by general readers, including those in the wider world of scholarship, which is otherwise disconnected from the closed community of Middle Eastern studies and the Middle East itself.

It is for this last reason that biographers and students of self-narrative working in a Middle Eastern medium have an outside chance to move their wider disciplines. Since so many disciplines burned their bridges to biography and the analysis of self-narrative, the present work of reconstruction is still open to all. Students of the Middle East again might arrive on the scene too late, and with too little equipment. But those who are inspired by the riveting tension of Middle Eastern lives perhaps hold a key to the inspiration of others.

1 First-Person Narrative in the Middle East

Bernard Lewis

AFTER the Young Turk Revolution of 1908, there was a sudden outpouring of something that had long been rare: the writing and publication of memoirs. Two new circumstances combined to produce this flowering of the memoir. The first was an interval of freedom of expression and publication in Turkey that had no precedent in the past and very few parallels in the future. The second was the urgent need felt by a number of rather senior and important figures to provide some explanation of what they had been doing during the previous thirty years. And so we find Said Pasha, grand vezir and holder of various other offices under Abdülhamid, producing three volumes of self-exculpatory memoirs; Kâmil Pasha, colleague and rival, doing the same; Said Pasha then producing comments on Kâmil Pasha's memoirs; Kâmil Pasha producing comments on Said Pasha's memoirs; and each producing a reply to the other's comments as well as to comments by a number of lesser mortals. Memoir writing engaged not only pashas but even some of the revolutionary leaders. Some of these works were translated from Turkish into Arabic and helped to set afoot a similar trend in the Arabic-speaking world.

It has been claimed that this was the beginning of memoir writing in the Near Eastern Muslim world and that until that time it was not the practice for people to write about themselves. It has been remarked that, generally speaking, the tendency among writers of history in Arabic was to conceal their own personalities, and it is noteworthy that when inserting a personal testimony, they often do so in the third person. Tabari, for example, the great medieval historian, when wishing to make a comment or observation of his own, says *qultu,* "I said," instead of his usual narrative introduction *qala,* "he said." But when he is producing a piece of evidence of his own, he says "*qala* Abu Jarir," this being his own sobriquet, thus distinguishing between information provided by him and comment made by him.

The idea that autobiographical writing, first-person writing, memoir writing, whatever we may choose to call it, begins with the Young Turk Revolution is quite mistaken. Such writing goes back a very long time, and I shall try to demonstrate this by putting before you a sort of prospectus of the different types of first-person narrative that have at one time or another flourished in this region and that have contributed directly or indirectly to the growth of memoir and autobiography in modern times.

First-person narrative figures among the most ancient writings of the Middle East and therefore in the world. Amenemhet of Egypt, of the twelfth dynasty that flourished between 1991 and 1962 B.C., wrote some rather interesting autobiographical texts. In a description of a journey to the south and some campaigns, each paragraph begins with "I did this" or "I did that," the classical approach of the autobiographer. Even more remarkable is an autobiographical inscription from a Hittite king, Hatusilis, who felt called on in about 1275 B.C. to provide a justification for his accession to the throne. He felt, almost uniquely among ancient and indeed more-recent rulers, that having obtained power to the disadvantage of other members of his own family, he had to provide a moral and legal justification for what he had done. So we have this rather strange spectacle of an ancient Hittite king saying in effect, "Well, I had to do this. It's true he was my brother . . ."

Another example is Tiglat Pileser, the Assyrian king who, writing about 1115 B.C., produced another of the classical types of first-person narrative; describing the innumerable countries he had conquered, cities he had devastated, and peoples he had killed or enslaved, thereby building up great glory for himself. Darius, the king of Persia, gives us another type in his Behistun inscription of about 520 B.C. that begins with his pedigree: his father, his grandfather, his ancestors.

When we pass from these and other for the most part now extinct Middle Eastern societies to that of the Jews, we have a somewhat different situation. In the Hebrew Bible, normally only God speaks in the first person. Normally, but not exclusively; there are exceptions. The Book of Deuteronomy, for example, is for the most part first-person narrative by Moses, or at least is presented as such, although it is hardly autobiographical. There are first-person passages in some of the Prophets and a genuine autobiography in the Book of Nehemiah, a personal statement of personal history probably unique in the ancient world. Another Jewish example is the autobiography of Josephus, written or at least surviving in Greek, in which he justifies his own rather questionable activities. M. Vidal Nacquet, the French classicist, described this as a manual of correct behavior in treason. Josephus gives us a perhaps classical example (classical because it was in Greek) of the self-justificatory memoir, explaining his life because it was necessary to answer a whole series of charges and accusations brought against him.

One interesting feature of Josephus's autobiography is that he begins with his pedigree. Apart from Darius, this is almost unique in antiquity. As far as I know, no other Greek or Latin author does so, and there are quite a number of autobiographical writings in Latin and Greek. Josephus begins with his ancestry, explaining that among the Jews, unlike other people, nobility is measured by priesthood, and he goes on to develop this theme at length. This practice of beginning with a pedigree became standard in Islamic times.

Of all the pre-Islamic societies that flourished in the Middle East, the one with the most recent and direct influence on early Islam was of course that of Iran. Unfortunately, we do not know a great deal about the literature of Iran in the period immediately preceding the advent of Islam, that is, in the Sasanid period, but we do have some information, including three documents that purport to be autobiographical and that survive in Arabic. One of them, ascribed to the Sasanid emperor Khusraw Anushirvan and preserved by Ibn Miskawayh, sets forth certain guiding principles that Khusraw as a king found it expedient to follow. This text is a mirror for princes, of a type common in Islamic literature, but is projected back into a pre-Islamic past and presented in the first person in the name of Khusraw; it is obviously not to be taken seriously as autobiography. Somewhat more autobiographical is a letter of advice from another Sasanid, Khusru Parviz, to his son Shiroye. This does make some personal statements and may in part be authentic.

Much more important than either of these is the brief auto-biography of Burzoye, a Persian physician who was sent to India, knew Indian languages, and translated from Sanskrit the collection of animal fables that later came to be known as *Kalila wa-Dimna.* The introduction to his autobiography states that the king gave orders to set down the history of this man from the day of his birth, including his education, his studies, his travels, "until his heart was filled with all kinds of wisdom and knowledge." As we shall see, this short autobiography became the model for a vast number of autobiographical writings— fragments rather than autobiographies—by men of learning.

Having set the scene, I come to the heart of my presentation, namely, the Islamic period. For convenience of rapid treatment and at the cost of some inevitable oversimplification, we may divide first-person writings into certain major classes, the first of which I would designate by the Arabic term *fakhr,* the boast. Perhaps the earliest Arabic autobiography is the *Mu'allaqa* of Imr al-Qays, and to a lesser extent some of the other "hanging odes" of ancient Arabia. These are often lengthy first-person statements describing deeds done. Quite a number of other fragments survive from ancient Arabia; the stories of the *Ayyam al-'Arab,* and other ancient poems are often markedly autobiographical.

This kind of personal statement of deeds done finds expression in an impressive number of royal memoirs, written personally by rulers or under their immediate direction. A fascinating example comes from the far west of Islam. 'Abdallah Ibn Buluggin, of the Zirid dynasty of Arabized Berbers who lived in the eleventh century, wrote a book-length account of life at court during his father's and his own lifetimes. A still better known autobiography is that of Usama ibn Munqidh, a local ruler in northern Syria in the twelfth century, who wrote what is probably the most informative single book in Arabic about what life was like in Syria at the time of the Crusades and what kind of human relationships existed between Muslims and Crusaders.

Such writings appear more frequently in the Persian than in the Arab or Turkish world. There are the pseudomemoirs of Timur, the genuine memoirs of Babar and of Tahmasp, and the still later first-person narratives of Nasir al-Din Shah. In contrast, the Ottoman sultans do not seem to have gone in for this kind of writing. They preferred to express themselves artistically by writing verse rather than memoirs. All the Ottoman sultans without exception composed poetry, and some of them were even poets.

Associated with the royal memoir is a rather special genre: the autobiographical biography, a book written by someone who is primarily a literary figure, who is closely associated with the ruler, and who writes a book that is at the same time a biography of the ruler and an autobiography of the writer, the two stories being commingled in order to show, among other things, the intimate position of the writer with the ruler. The best example of this genre is 'Imad al-Din's book about his life with Saladin. If he had been modern, he might have called it "My Life with Saladin" or "Saladin and I"; he actually called it *al-Barq al-Shami*. Displaying at times an almost epic quality, it is a remarkably informative document about Saladin and also about 'Imad al-Din. About the same time, 'Umara al-Yamani, a courtier of the last Fatimid rulers of Egypt, a minor poet and a man of letters, wrote an autobiographical work that is also of considerable interest.

The first category of first-person narrative consists, then, of "things that I did." The second category might be defined as "places I went to and things I saw." In the Middle East, there is an extensive travel literature, arising from many different kinds of travel. Medieval Islamic society enjoyed a far greater degree of voluntary, personal mobility than did any other known premodern society. Men, and sometimes women, traveled; they planned, organized, and conducted long journeys.

The main impetus, of course, was the Muslim pilgrimage, which requires every Muslim once in a lifetime, whether living in Morocco, in Java, in Central Asia, in Central Africa, to go to the Hijaz, visit the holy places, and join with other Muslims in certain rites. An elaborate system of arrangements all over the Muslim world facilitated the pilgrimage. There were roads, relay stations, and other services, and we know of a large number of individual travelers. The pilgrimage became associated with other forms of travel, notably travel for trade and travel for study. Scholars went to study under different teachers: "Seek for learning even in China," says a *hadith*. This is not meant in any sense to be derogatory to China; it simply means that even if you have to go that far, still go. This whole category of writings is devoted to "journeys I made, places I visited, teachers at whose feet I sat, whose courses I attended, whose lectures I noted down," and the like. People collected shaykhs, and books that are "shaykhs under whom I studied" form a recognized genre, the *mashyakha*.

There were also diplomatic envoys who, exceptionally, had interesting things to say. There were captives who managed to get themselves ransomed and returned home. And, in more modern times, there were students who went abroad and came back with often very strange stories.

One of the earliest of these travelers was an Arab called Harun ibn Yahya, who was taken prisoner and sent first to Constantinople and then to Rome in about 886. He wrote a brief description of Rome and Western Europe that was preserved by a later geographer. Others, including such famous figures as Ibn Battuta (whose descriptions of the world are at least in part written in the first person), recounted personal adventures and experiences, personal contacts and relationships, conversations with other people, and personal reactions to the strange and wonderful things that they found.

In the Ottoman period we have accounts of India, such as that of the admiral Sidi Ali Reis, who went to India in the late sixteenth century. We have a number of Ottoman ambassadors to Europe, to Iran, to Central Asia, to India, and we have the unique and incomparable Evliya Chelebi, who died in 1684 and wrote of a whole series of adventures. Unfortunately one of the problems with Evliya Chelebi is his credibility. To call him a liar, as some have done, is an injustice; he makes it quite clear in the introduction to his book that his purpose is to entertain rather than to instruct. He is indeed one of the few authors who tells us why he is writing the book and what he is trying to accomplish. There is undoubtedly a great deal of personal information in his work. His account of Vienna, where he went as a member of the entourage of an Ottoman ambassador, is particularly interesting. He seems to have spent some time in the city, and the responses of an Ottoman gentleman to imperial Vienna in the seventeenth century make a remarkable document.

In the nineteenth century, the literature of travel acquired a new dimension with the process of European discovery and the growing number of students, then diplomatic envoys, and then political exiles who visited the lands beyond Islam. To these three major groups, we may add royal visitors.

If the first two categories are "what I did" and "what I saw," the third, more interesting in many ways, is concerned with "what I thought." These latter works are rarely book length. Most are short statements by scientists and philosophers, apparently written for inclusion in some larger biographical work. Reference has already been made to the existence in Arabic and later, to a much lesser extent, in Persian and Turkish of vast biographical dictionaries. Scholars were obviously concerned to have a proper and correct entry in these medieval versions of *Who's Who,* and some of them took care to provide an outline. Thus when Ibn Abi Usaybi'a compiled his famous biographical dictionary of physicians, many of the physicians in his book provided their own biographies directly. Quite a number of remarkable personal statements by medieval physicians are included in this and other biographical dictionaries, and some entries are preserved from earlier periods. From as early as 873, we have a kind of memoir by Hunayn ibn Ishaq, a translator, who talks about his work, his rivals, and his critics; a memoir by the great physician Muhammad ibn Zakariya al-Razi, who died in 925; and another by an Egyptian physician called Ibn Ridwan, who tells the heartbreaking story of his impoverished childhood and hard times, his inability to study properly because he had no money, and his success in completing his studies all the same: an intensely personal statement also offered as a moral lesson for others.

Not only the scientists and philosophers wrote in this manner, but also others with a more specifically religious purpose, and notably the Sufis. Muhasibi (d. 857) is an example. Hallaj left some autobiographical fragments. These writers want to tell us of their mystical experiences, for our enlightenment and for our guidance. Surely the outstanding and classical example of the religious autobiography in Islamic literature is Ghazali's (d. 1111) *Saviour from Error.* In it he tells of his struggle to achieve a true understanding of the world, the universe, and the predicament of humankind. He speaks of trying the way of the philosopher, the way of the theologian, and finding that each one was unsatisfactory. He finally found the true way, that of the mystic, and through that, with some changes, he managed to achieve the understanding that he sought. Among scholars, this introspection takes the different forms of autobibliography and what might be called autohagiography; an outstanding example of the latter is Sha'rani (d. 1565).

One religious autobiography is of particular interest, that by an Ismaili *da'i,* or propagandist, who worked in Iraq in the interest of the Fatimid caliph. He was a propaganda agent of subversion and influence in the territories ruled by the Buyids and eventually was recalled to headquarters in Cairo where, if I may translate it into modern language, he became first a high official in the ministry of propaganda and then minister of propaganda—the head of the *Da'wa,* or *da'i al-du'at.* His narrative, one of the very rare book-length autobiographies, is a curious mixture of personal statement, religious testimony, and career intrigue. It consists of debates that he had with other people, speeches that he made, sermons that he delivered, letters that he wrote, and actions that he took—demonstrating how clever he was in various tricky diplomatic situations. In the last part, when he is in Cairo and working in the Fatimid government, he tells of his disagreements with other people and describes how this one and that one were treacherous and dishonest, or stupid and vicious, and how he got things right and was therefore deserving of credit and attention. This is the most modern of these books, an early prototype of the present-day memoir that consists of speeches, letters, debates and experiences, accusations against one's rivals, and above all self-justification.

I spoke a moment ago of the autobibliography. These became more and more common as the biographical dictionaries became larger, more capacious, more copious, and more numerous. Roughly from the thirteenth century onward, there were great numbers of short autobiographies and short memoirs— half a page, a page, rarely much more—that were someone's draft for his own *Who's Who* entry. More often than not, such entries were provided to disciples who then included them in their books. These disciples and compilers also offered self-portraits. The biographical dictionaries were normally arranged chronologically by years of death, and the individual entries were therefore not, so to speak, published until after the subject's death. But some compilers arranged their entries by the centuries in which they flourished and therefore felt able to include themselves in their own biographical dictionaries. Sometimes they spoke of themselves in the third person, a practice shared with such distinguished figures as Julius Caesar and

Charles de Gaulle; at other times, they wrote in the first person. Some of these accounts are mixed, as for example that of the famous Ibn Tulun of Syria; he begins his autobiography in the third person and halfway through switches to the first person. An outstanding book that combines many of these different features is the autobiography of the great Ibn Khaldun. This is not strictly speaking a book but part of a book, a book-length component in his vast universal history. In this he talks of his ancestry, his education, the shaykhs under whom he studied, his travels, his writings, his career, and his scholarship. It is certainly the most comprehensive and, as one would expect from Ibn Khaldun, intellectually the most interesting and the most satisfying.

A distinct group consists of autobiographies by those who lived in some sense on the margins of Islamic society, for example, the *dhimmis,* non-Muslims living within the Muslim community who, for one reason or another, wrote memoirs or statements about themselves. Two Jewish figures are credited with probably apocryphal autobiographies, Eldad Hadani and David Reubeni; an interesting eighteenth-century figure from Jerusalem, Azulay, produced a real autobiography. Among Christians, there were several memoir writers in the nineteenth century, including Mikha'il Mishaqqa, Rustum Baz, and Arutin.

Some of these non-Muslims were converts to Islam. The Jew known as Samuel al-Maghribi was converted in 1163 and wrote a refutation of Judaism called *Ifham al-Yahud,* to which he appended a brief statement about himself and his family, explaining that he had postponed his conversion because he did not want to distress his father. Ahmad Faris al-Shidyaq wrote extensive memoirs; an experienced convert, he became a Protestant first and then a Muslim.

A special genre consists of solicited memoirs, those written on request, usually of someone European, someone from outside the Islamic world. Some of these documents are interesting personal statements, in part because of the circumstances that brought them into existence. The Yemeni Jew Hayyim Habshush, for example, who escorted Halévy in his travels in the Yemen, was asked twenty years later by Edward Glaser to write memoirs of himself and Halévy. Habshush wrote a kind of autobiographical cum biographical travel book, a kind of *al-Barq al-Shami* on a small scale. There was an Egyptian shaykh called Tantawi who somehow found his way to Russia where he died in 1861, but not before becoming one of the founders of the Russian School of Arabic Studies. Tantawi was asked by a Russian Orientalist of the time to write an autobiography, which he obligingly did. There was the Ottoman interpreter known as Mütercim Osman, a native of Temesvár, at that time an Ottoman city, who was in the service of the Pasha of Temesvár. Osman knew several languages, as apparently did everybody in Temesvár. He spoke Serbian and Hungarian as well as Turkish; after his capture by the Austrians in war, he spent eleven years in captivity during which he mastered German. He was then ransomed or exchanged and went home and got an excellent job as chief interpreter to the Pasha of Temesvár. He wrote two volumes of memoirs, fascinating books about the Turko-Austrian wars in and around Hungary. What is still more interesting is that each of these volumes survives only in a single manuscript, one in Vienna, the other at the British Museum, and that the work is totally unknown to Ottoman historiography or literature.

In the nineteenth century, again, a number of people wrote memoirs to order: Khayr al-Din al-Tunisi, for example, who was asked to write in French; As'ad Khayat, who wrote in English; and a rather curious person known as Mme. Veuve Kibrisli Mehmet Pasha, the widow of Kibrisli Mehmet Pasha, whose book, written or at least published in English in 1872, contains the remarkable memoirs of an Ottoman lady.

What sort of pattern, if any, emerges from this kind of first-person writing, memoirs, autobiographical fragments, and the like, of which I have selected merely the high points? Certain things are almost standard. These writers begin with ancestry, although in Greco-Roman antiquity only Josephus does so. In Islamic autobiographical writing, this opening is practically universal and includes as many generations as possible. In extreme cases people will go back to Adam, but certainly as far back as ancient Arabia. They say where they were born, though not necessarily when they were born. (There seems to be a certain vanity that inhibits some of our memoirists from giving the date of their birth.) The place of birth is important, and some words of praise for the beauties of the place are often included, perhaps the citation of a well-known *hadith, Hubb al-watan min al-iman,* love of one's birthplace is part of the faith, and the like. Then, particularly among the scholarly autobiographies, education and travels follow, forming a kind of curriculum vitae. This section may include "the books I have read and the books I have written," and if the autobiography or fragment is a religious one, then of course the religious experience. The length varies enormously. Relatively few are separate books or even long enough to form separate books. The great majority are brief, running from a few lines to a few pages, and obviously written for inclusion in some larger book, either one's own or someone else's.

Finally, why? What are the purposes of these writings? Here again, at the risk of oversimplifying, I would put them in three main categories: to serve oneself, to serve others, and to serve posterity. To serve oneself covers, of course, the numerous apologia written to justify what one has already done or to facilitate what one hopes to do next. The two purposes are often linked. To serve others refers in particular to the religious works. There is no doubt about the religious sincerity of Ghazali or of Avicenna in writing for the intellectual guidance of their readers. And posterity is the intended audience of those who are concerned about their place in history, an important concern in Sunni Islam where, by the very nature of Sunni beliefs, the sense of history is strongly developed.

In the course of the nineteenth century, under the influence of European models, many memoirs of one kind or another were added. In the twentieth century, they have become an unstoppable torrent.

2 Traditional Islamic Learning and Ideas of the Person in the Twentieth Century

Dale F. Eickelman

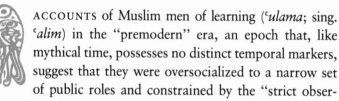ACCOUNTS of Muslim men of learning (*'ulama*; sing. *'alim*) in the "premodern" era, an epoch that, like mythical time, possesses no distinct temporal markers, suggest that they were oversocialized to a narrow set of public roles and constrained by the "strict observance of traditionally established behavior patterns."[1] A presumed consequence of tradition is that men of learning, imbued with central cultural and social roles in premodern Muslim societies, lacked the disposition and opportunity to sustain these roles in the modern world and thus have become the equivalent of an endangered species. This essay argues that the discontinuity between past men of learning and those of the present is primarily an artifact of "ulamology," to use L. Carl Brown's deliberate neologism. The religious traditions sustained by ulama and the response of these customs to changing political and economic circumstances have been more flexible than the self-image sustained by men of learning themselves.

The capacity of traditionally educated religious intellectuals to play decisive contemporary roles is evident in postrevolutionary Iran, where Ayatollah Khomeini rivaled Ronald Reagan as a "great communicator" by using the mass media and Friday sermons in innovative ways to influence a large and diverse audience, an impact sustained by his clerical successors. Men of learning also remain politically significant in the Arab Middle East.[2] Far from fading away in colonial North Africa, men of learning adapted to radically altered circumstances, although not as a bloc. Ulama in French Algeria were innovators and conservatives, liberals and reactionaries. Some withdrew from participation in colonial institutions, others opposed them, and still others saw certain colonial reforms as offering the possibility for revitalizing the Muslim community.[3] In Morocco, the cooperation of judges, advisors, and administrators was vital in establishing and maintaining colonial rule. After independence in 1956, Moroccan ulama remained an important component of the elite, and their support of the monarchy is important still in maintaining popular political legitimacy. This is also true elsewhere in the Muslim world.[4]

Self-Images of Men of Learning: Morocco and Oman

The principal vehicle for self-representation of men of learning is the *tarjama,* which in Arabic can mean both biography and autobiography. The term dates from at least the tenth century.[5] Using accounts drawn from opposite ends of the Arab world, Morocco and Oman, I argue that tarjamas, often neglected because of their highly stylized and seemingly inflexible features, serve as an index of changes in self-representation with the important qualification that tarjamas cannot be considered independently of the social contexts for which they are produced. In both Morocco and Oman, I am concerned with persons in regional settings rather than those at the highest levels of political authority.

Islam is a literate and complex civilization, but until recently the vast majority of Muslims has lacked direct access to the written word. In Morocco over 90 percent of the population was illiterate through the 1950s; in Oman this was the case through the 1970s. Since then, significant strides have been made in educating the school-age population in both societies, although literacy rates for the adult population remain low. In both countries, literacy has been primarily associated with religious learning, but this has begun to change: state schooling now affords more prestige to diplomas in other fields. Nonetheless, the popular link between literacy and religious status remains strong. Although a reputation for religious learning does not guarantee high social status, it usually implies wealth, leadership, and distinguished descent.[6]

Individual and Person

The distinction between "individual" and "person" is useful in discerning how traditional Muslim religious scholars represent their social roles. "Individual" refers to the mortal human being, the object of observation and self-reflection. Thus individuals can wield considerable power and still not be recognized as playing a significant or legitimate social role. "Person" refers to the cultural concepts that lend social significance to the individual. Personhood can be regarded as a status that "varies according to social criteria which contain the capacities of the individual within defined roles and categories."[7] The notion of "person," to paraphrase Jean La Fontaine, is society's confirmation that an individual's identity has social significance.

The roles and categories of the person are defined by society. As Marcel Mauss reminds us, persona in ancient Rome was literally a person's social mask, a locus of general rights and duties. In clan-based societies, such as ancient Rome, the role of the person was to act out "the prefigured totality of the life of the clan," allowing very little room for individuality.[8] Mauss's distinction between individual—he used the term "self"—and person contains an evolutionary assumption: the rise of Christianity saw the emergence of the "moral person," a growing fusion between the person in the sense of social roles and masks and the self as a conscious, metaphysical entity. He argues that other societies, including such "ancient" (and in his view static) civilizations as India and China, possessed fixed categories of person that ceased to evolve.[9]

Orientalist scholars attributed to Muslim societies a similar fixed nature, of which one component was men of learning with less autonomy and personal responsibility than their counterparts in Western societies. Yet, from the beginning of Islam in seventh-century Arabia, Muslim doctrine has stressed personal responsibility and autonomy. The Qurʾanic vision of person-God relations is devoid of intermediaries, although many seventh-century sources depict a tension between Qurʾanic notions of person and other ones. The historian al-Tabari (d. 923), for example, relates that a member of the B. Rabiʿa tribal confederation posed several questions to Musaylima bin Habib, a B. Rabiʿa rival of Muhammad. After questioning Musaylima, the tribesman concluded "that Muhammad is telling the truth. But a liar of the Rabiʿa is better for us than a true prophet of the Mudar." (A more skeptical version of the same account is, "A liar of the Rabiʿa is better than a liar of the Mudar.")[10] In both versions, loyalty to the collectivity takes precedence over the obligation of the individual to God. We shall return to the issue of the coexistence of competing notions of person and individual and to situations in which only some individuals can realize a full sense of person.

The emergence of the self as an explicit subject in biographies and autobiographies has been an important element of Western social thought since the eighteenth century. Indeed, the idea of the self, a conscious and self-reflexive "me" or "I" possessing individuality and an "inner" life, is so integral to modern European thought that it is considered a natural part of the social landscape.

Tarjamas

A tarjama is generally written in the third person, even if autobiographical, suggesting a distancing from self, an appeal to set standards and understandings. The components include a genealogy, an account of formal education and Qur'anic memorization, a list of teachers (often including close relatives, which indicates family support for religious learning), the books and subjects studied, and selections from the subject's poetry, aphorisms, or other contributions to learning. Dates are provided whenever possible, since the ability to date events distinguishes the traditionally educated from the unlearned.

Tarjamas purport to represent words and deeds reliably and with credible witnesses. Quotation marks are not used, and the stylistic tag, "he said to him" (*qal lu*), does not clearly distinguish between speech and paraphrase. The tarjama records the evidence of a person's character and actions; it contains no speculation concerning "inner" self or motive other than anecdotes that demonstrate piety and devotion to Qur'anic studies.

These accounts record the persona of men of learning, the actions and attributes that legitimate their piety and scholarly authority. Other activities, no matter how significant for understanding the role of the individual, are not part of the reported scholarly persona. Marriages are not mentioned, and women are mentioned only when they encourage Qur'anic memorization and recital. In most instances, the family contexts in which early learning occurs cannot be directly ascertained from a tarjama unless the father or other relatives play a direct role in Qur'anic education.[11] Likewise, peer learning, a crucial element in understanding traditional education, is passed over in silence. The same is true for many political activities. Men of learning may be landlords, politicians, and shrewd entrepreneurs, but these activities are outside the scope of the tarjama, which concentrates on those elements of personhood that link individuals with the sacred center of society, as viewed in religious terms.

There have always been alternative forms of biography and self-representation, ranging from the life of the Prophet (*sirat*) and the chronicles of caliphs and rulers to the lives and miracles of saints, pilgrimage accounts, and, since at least the early nineteenth century, memoirs influenced by the Western genre. The third-person representation of Taha Husayn's autobiographical *The Stream of Days,* sometimes assumed to be a realistic image of an Egyptian childhood and mosque-school education, is influenced by European literary forms, as is Algerian Malek Bennabi's *Mémoires d'un témoin du siècle.*[12] The Moroccan ʿAllal al-Fasi (d. 1974), a popular lecturer at the Qarawiyin mosque-university in Fez in the early 1930s and subsequently a key leader in the nationalist movement, spoke only Arabic, yet the style of his autobiographical writings suggests the influence of forms beyond those of the Qarawiyin.[13]

Tarjamas represent religious scholars to specific, known audiences. Indeed, for a younger generation with a "modern" education, the term tarjama and the form of religious authority it represents often go unrecognized.[14] Until the availability of printing in the nineteenth century for Morocco and the 1970s for the Omani interior, tarjamas circulated only in manuscript form; access to them depended on networks of ulama. Even after the introduction of printing, tarjamas continued to circulate in this form. The compilation of Mukhtar al-Susi cited above circulated for at least two decades prior to its publication in 1961; in Oman several compilations continue to circulate only as manuscripts.

There are several points of resemblance between tarjamas in Oman and Morocco. In both tarjama traditions, genealogies link men of learning with their distinguished ancestors, and the enumeration of scholars under whom the subjects studied does the same for their claims to scholarly authority. Selections from the subjects' sayings and actions exemplify character, lists of distinguished students represent their continued authority, and the sayings of associates who admire them enhance authority.

Tarjamas are not ordered by a chronological sequence of events, although genealogical descent and the details of early studies usually come first. Anecdotes intended to show character do not distinguish between youth or maturity. Because the personas of men of learning are linked to fixed qualities, sequence and chronology become peripheral. Indeed, the material chosen for the tarjamas analyzed here suggests that the primary audience is contemporary and not an abstract, generalized audience of future generations.

The Maghrib

In Morocco as in Oman, it is difficult to separate a tarjama from its intended audience. A tarjama is almost always prepared in response to a specific request, often for inclusion in one of the compilations that reveal complex, mutually supportive networks of patronage among men of learning. Mukhtar as-Susi's *al-Maʿsul* portrays judges, court functionaries, teachers, and others with claims to learning as regularly offering hospitality and gifts to writers of such compendia, to poets, and to others who could enhance their reputations.

The three Moroccan tarjamas discussed here indicate significant situational differences, although they share the problem of reconciling Muslim identity with participation in colonial rule. The ulama discussed in two of these tarjamas are brothers, Ahmad Mansuri (1895–1975) and ʿAbd al-Rahman Mansuri (b. 1912), from Bzu, a Berber village not far from Marrakesh. The third tarjama is by a former chief judge of Tangier, Ahmad bin ʿAbd al-Salam al-Bu ʿAyyashi (1910–83).[15]

The Mansuri brothers' tarjamas lack specific genealogies; neither brother goes further back than their paternal grandfather. In the late nineteenth century, their father, Mansur bin Ahmad (d. 1946), fled from a village in the High Atlas Mountains because an intertribal dispute threatened his life. He settled in Bzu and attained a quasimaraboutic status among local tribespeople. He was a notary, a devout member of the Kittaniya religious order, and by the early twentieth century a minor landowner. ʿAbd al-Rahman relates various popular accounts of his father's piety and the efforts of some genealogical "specialists" who approached the brothers in the 1930s, when their reputations as notables were secure, with "evidence" of their descent from the Prophet Muhammad. None of this information appears in the tarjamas, although the tarjamas of other scholars characteristically make such claims. Not doing so was a means of indicating participation in the reform movements of the early twentieth century. Both brothers emphasize their credentials as men of learning over status based on descent.

Ahmad Mansuri

Ahmad Mansuri's tarjama describes his schooling (from 1913 to 1919). He names his teachers, specifies where he studied (a tent school in a hamlet near Bzu and the Yusufiya mosque-university in Marrakesh), and cites the texts memorized or commented on. He mentions his brief teaching career in Bzu, but not his financial support for students from the Bzu region to continue their religious studies at the Yusufiya.

In 1919 the French native affairs officer for the Bzu region asked Ahmad to assist in the "pacification" of the Ait ʿTab, a large tribe in an adjacent region. Ahmad also assisted in establishing the region's first agricultural tax (tartib). His tarjama records these facets of his career, commenting only that he cooperated with the French to avoid unnecessary bloodshed. He omits the protectorate's award of a medal for bravery, the Ouissam al-Harb.

French authorities again requested Ahmad's assistance in 1925 in Azilal, a nearby regional center. When he returned to Bzu at the end of the year, he was appointed qadi, a post he

held until 1953 when he was removed for his refusal to recognize the French deposition and exile of Sultan Muhammad V.
Ahmad's tarjama records that a French native affairs officer,
who had known him from earlier years, intervened to prevent
confiscation of his property and a prison sentence, the fate of
other notables who opposed the deposition. In the tumultuous
years following independence in 1956, Ahmad briefly served as
both qadi (in 1956 and 1957) and district officer, or qaʾid
(1956). Later he was appointed to the prestigious Constitu-
tional Council (1960) and won election to Morocco's first par-
liament (1963).

Qadi Ahmad's correct relations with French authorities, although by no means deferential or obsequious, figure in his tarjama. Cooperation is justified in the "heroic" years of colonial
"penetration" as a matter of avoiding greater collective harm;
thereafter it is noted as an activity that the French obliged him
to do, and he is thus freed of personal responsibility.

ʿAbd al-Rahman Mansuri

The tarjama of ʿAbd al-Rahman, Qadi Ahmad's younger
brother, places emphasis on his education rather than on his
judicial career. He memorized the Qurʾan (completed "when
he was aged twelve to fifteen") and studied at tent schools near
Bzu and Azilal, where, like his elder brother, he first learned
Arabic. He studied in Azilal in 1925 when his brother was there
assisting the French. The tarjama records Ahmad's presence in
Azilal as a clerk (katib).

ʿAbd al-Rahman's tarjama ends in April 1935, when he was
compelled to break off his studies and return to Bzu to serve as
his brother's deputy in order to prevent the unpaid post from

going to an outsider. A separate diary, kept intermittently from his return to Bzu until his 1957 appointment as qadi in Boujad, provides a record of events after 1935. (Some parts of the diary were destroyed to avoid arrest in the final years of the French protectorate.) The diary records marriages, property titles related to the Mansuri brothers, lists of wedding guests, the visits of notables and men of learning to Bzu, the prices and availability of foodstuffs and commodities during the 1940s, droughts, epidemics, French regulations and exactions, and the Allied invasion.

The events in the diary, unlike events recorded in the tarjama, were outside ʿAbd al-Rahman's public persona as a man of learning. Even the act of recording was problematic. As he explained, such things were best passed by word of mouth among trusted confidants, through chains of known, reliable witnesses, and written about only in obscure language to avoid political complications; for politics, oral sources were more reliable than written ones, and the oral tradition shared by men of learning provides the background necessary to understand the significance of such events.

A Nationalist Judge

Ahmad al-Bu ʿAyyashi's tarjama shows a developed awareness of alternative literary forms. He published, at his own expense, a history of ʿAbd al-Krim al-Khattabi's Rifian revolt (1923–27) and a play, never performed, on the nationalist struggle. Bu ʿAyyashi's father was tribal leader of the Bani Waryajil until his death in 1946 and minister of defense in ʿAbd al-Krim al-Khattabi's Rifian Republic.

The genealogical section of Bu ʿAyyashi's tarjama begins with a discussion of the proper name in Arabic for the Bani Waryajil (Ait Waryaghar in Rifian Berber), and he opts for Arabic on the grounds that the tribe was an "early" adherent to Islam. He traces his descent from Musa bin Haddu, a twelfth-century marabout from the Bani ʿAyyash, the subgroup that provided leadership for the Bani Waryajil for several centuries. Because Bu ʿAyyashi emphasizes the Bani ʿAyyash's role in the struggle against colonial rule, his genealogy cites his twelfth-century maraboutic ancestor and skips directly to his paternal grandfather (d. 1900 or 1901), ruler (*hakim*) of the tribe, a pious man who applied much of his "vast" wealth to rearm his tribe for resistance to Spanish rule. Bu ʿAyyashi then discusses his father's role in the Rifian Republic.

Bu ʿAyyashi's account of his early studies is perfunctory. He includes his stay at the Qarawiyin mosque-university in Fez from 1929 to 1936 but mentions only teachers who became important in the nationalist movement, tutored Morocco's present monarch, or became senior officials after independence. The subjects he studied are mentioned generally, and no specific texts are cited. In 1936 he went on the pilgrimage as part of a quasi-official Moroccan delegation carrying a message from Sultan Muhammad V to ʿAbd al-ʿAziz ibn Saʿud. The delegation was led by one of Bu ʿAyyashi's teachers, a former minister of justice in Morocco's French zone, who was dismissed by the French in 1930 for opposing the "Berber decree" that restricted the application of Islamic law in Morocco's Berber regions.

Bu ʿAyyashi's tarjama is more elaborate in citing connections to persons in the nationalist movement than to those noted for their learning. As in Ahmad Mansuri's case, he records as an event beyond his control his appointment by the Spanish as Bani Waryajil qadi. After the outbreak of the Spanish Civil War, colonial authorities imprisoned Bu ʿAyyashi's father as a guarantee for his tribe's good conduct and his own return from Fez, as well as to forestall renewed anti-Spanish violence. Bu ʿAyyashi claims that his work as a qadi insulated him from collaboration. He describes his relationship to Spanish authorities as that of "old adversaries who have spent considerable time together." In 1939, he became a member of the Council for Higher Education in Tetouan, capital of the former Spanish zone, and when the zone was incorporated into independent Morocco in early 1957, he served briefly as a regional administrator (qaʾid mumtaz) in the ministry of the interior. He felt uncomfortable in an explicitly political role, however, and requested a transfer to the ministry of justice, where he served as a criminal court judge until his retirement in 1976.

Bu ʿAyyashi details his activities in the late 1940s and early 1950s, when the nationalist movement acquired popular momentum, as characterized by bureaucratic infighting with colonial authorities, internal disputes among pronationalist Bani Waryajil lineages and their opposition, and the difficulties of openly supporting the nationalist movement and functioning as qadi at the same time. In interviews, although not in the tarjama, he said that he reconciled these roles by speaking publicly in a way that could be read as nationalist by the nationalists but remained sufficiently ambiguous so that Spanish authorities could not document opposition to their authority. The tarjama provides extracts from these speeches.

Oman and the Ibadiyya

There are major differences in scale between Morocco and Oman. Oman's current population is just over a million, of which some 20 percent are foreign workers, while Morocco's population is over twenty-four million. Morocco's most important economic transformations have occurred gradually since the early part of the century; for Oman the most crucial period has been occasioned by the intensified search for oil in the early 1950s, its discovery in commercial quantities in 1964, its export beginning in 1967, and the 1970 palace coup, which saw the application of oil revenues to education, security, and development projects. Moroccan Muslims are all Sunni and follow the Maliki legal school; Omanis are more diverse.

Oman's pluralism offers a contrast to nonsectarian Morocco. Almost all Omani nationals are Muslim (although a handful of Hindu merchants with ties to the palace have been granted Omani citizenship), but there are important sectarian distinctions among the Muslim population. The Ibadiyya account for 40–45 percent of Oman's citizen population and predominate in the mountainous northern interior of the country. From 1913 to 1955, the Ibadi tribes of the interior broke away from rule by the Al Bu Saʿid dynasty and were autonomously governed by an imam selected by men of learning and tribal leaders. Sunni Muslims form a majority on the coast and in the southern region of Dhufar, where they constitute 50–55 percent of the population. However, significant distinctions exist between the Sunni of the north and those of the south. Men of learning in the south form an almost hereditary stratum of society, as was the case for the Hadramawt region of southern

Yemen, where Dhufar's Sunni men of learning received their religious training until the 1960s when political turbulence severed this line of communication. Finally, the Shiᶜa, constituting less than 3 percent of Oman's population, are concentrated in the large coastal cities, including Suhar and Muscat. Added to this complexity is the fact that religious divisions in the coastal regions are crosscut linguistically and ethnically, with Sindi, Baluch, and Persian being the principal non-Arabic languages of northern Oman.

Men of learning in each community are seldom in regular contact with their counterparts in other sectarian groups. Until the early 1960s the intellectual ties of Dhufar's men of learning were with southern Yemen and not with their northern Omani counterparts. A further contributing factor was that Oman's ruler until 1970, Saᶜid bin Taymur, discouraged internal travel. The Sunni community in the north also looks outside of Oman. In Musandam Peninsula, the dominant lineage of the Kamaliyin has produced the leading religious scholars for generations. The post of qadi in Musandam's principal town, Khassab, has been held by a Kamali since at least the early part of this century, and other members of the lineage hold religious appointments in Kuwait and Abu Dhabi. The present qadi in Khassab, who succeeded his father in 1932, studied at a religious school on the Iranian island of Qeshem, located directly north of the Straits of Hormuz. Until the Iranian revolution, Qeshem and the mainland Iranian town of Lengeh were centers of learning for the Sunni (Shafiᶜi, to be precise), Arabic-speaking Muslims of the Gulf region, and they drew students from as far away as India. As of 1980 about seventy students remained there, most of the students leaving for Dubai after the outbreak of the Iran-

Iraq war. Elsewhere in coastal Oman, there is a similar external orientation among the Sunni community, at least for traditional religious studies. Family ties and links with centers of learning allow them considerable mobility but attenuate communication among different sectarian groups within Oman itself.

The same tendency toward autonomy prevails among Oman's Shiʿa. One example is the religious leader of one of the coastal Arabic-speaking Shiʿa communities. The son of a wealthy land-owner (who, the son said, would have been called a "feudalist" had he been an Iraqi), this shaykh studied in Najaf, Iraq, from 1969 until 1973 under Shaykh Muhammad Baqir al-Sadr (ex-ecuted by the Iraqi government in 1980) and subsequently in Qum, where he remained until political disturbances forced him to break off his studies.[16] Well read and articulate, this shaykh nonetheless indicated little direct knowledge of religious leaders in other sectarian groups except for those in his im-mediate locale.

Only Ibadi networks of learning are centered on Oman itself. Although there are Ibadi communities elsewhere in the world, the Ibadi of Oman have, for all practical purposes, been isolated from them. Prior to 1970, regular links were maintained only with the Ibadiyya of East Africa, most of whom are of Omani origin.

Until the 1960s, literacy in the Omani interior implied reli-gious learning and was widely respected, although its practical use as a means to economic or social advancement was limited. In principle, Qurʾanic and higher education was open to all, but in practice, regular participation was difficult without the support of relatives already familiar with the world of learning. Acquiring a reputation as a man of learning entailed sponsorship, and rhetorical skills could not be derived solely from the study of religious texts. Thus, scholars who were part of the tribal oligarchy or sponsored by it had a competitive advantage. Leading shaykhs conducted lesson circles, visited, challenged one another in poetry and aphorisms, and circulated manuscripts among themselves (and because manuscripts were copied by hand, considerable time and expense were involved in obtaining and commissioning copies; thus access was controlled and restricted). Reading was not an anonymous, solitary act, since religious manuscripts were usually read and commented on in small gatherings of men of learning.

Hamra³ al-ʿAbriyin, a tribal capital of the interior (not far from the old imamate capital of Nizwa), provides an example of the uses of literacy in the pre-1970 Omani interior. In the 1940s, the town had a population of 1,200. Of this number, one scholar possessed a country-wide reputation for learning. About thirty other individuals, most of them members of the shaykhly lineage that provided the tribal leadership, also possessed high levels of literacy. Yet no more than five of the thirty knew the conventions of Islamic law pertaining to inheritance, land transactions, and marriage well enough to prepare appropriate documents. Another fifty townspeople were able to read and write, in addition to being able to recite the Qurʾan. Except for the Qurʾan, a few standard religious texts, and the manuscripts that passed among the leading men of learning, virtually no books were available.

As in Morocco, a reputation as a man of learning was achieved primarily by word of mouth, since the small scale of society limited the scope for what had to be said in writing. No men of learning in the nineteenth- or twentieth-century Omani interior possessed formal written credentials, such as the *ijazas* that were common in Morocco and other parts of the Muslim world. In the small-scale society of the imamate, the number of men of learning was in the hundreds, and far fewer if only the upper ranks are considered.

The form taken by contemporary Ibadi tarjamas is indicated by a manuscript by Shaykh Ibrahim Saʿid al-ʿAbri (d. 1975) on the history of the ʿAbriyin tribe, prepared at the request of a leading man of learning of the interior who sought similar accounts from the learned men of other tribes.[17] Shaykh Ibrahim, like his counterparts elsewhere in the northern interior, was both a religious scholar and a man of action. He claims to have been responsible for persuading Muhammad ibn ʿAbd Allah al-Khalili to accept leadership as imam in 1920, a title he held until his death in 1954. For a number of years, Shaykh Ibrahim was both qadi and tribal leader of the ʿAbriyin, as well as a counselor of the imam. He also found time to teach almost daily. After 1937 he became qadi for the sultan, dividing his time between the sultanate and the imamate. After the 1970 coup that brought the son of the former ruler to power, Shaykh Ibrahim became Oman's first mufti, or official interpreter of Islamic jurisprudence.

Shaykh Ibrahim's manuscript spans four-hundred years of tribal history. The older sections are largely taken from earlier treatises, but Shaykh Ibrahim is clearly responsible for much of the nineteenth- and twentieth-century material. The account sometimes incorporates letters and other documents, which are not always ordered by chronology. The mention of a place associated with an early tribal migration prompts the inclusion of a famous poem recited there in his youth (e.g., p. 12), and a request that Shaykh Ibrahim write a tarjama of the father of a man of learning occasions Ibrahim's spirited refutation (using "I" for the only time in the manuscript) of charges that he defied the authority of the imam during a tribal dispute of the 1930s (pp. 111–33).

Genealogical links in a small-scale society like the Omani interior were public and widely known, so there was much less latitude in this region as compared to Morocco for reinventing the past. Men of learning were aware of the complex links of descent and alliance both within and between tribes. Ordinary tribespeople, although generally unable to express these links in great detail, knew their general outlines. These matters were decidedly important for tarjamas. Although men of learning were expected to rise above tribal loyalties in the service of the imam (for the pre-1955 period), in practice they acted on behalf of their tribes or were suspected of doing so. Accusations by Shaykh Ibrahim's detractors that he defied the imam, mentioned above, suggest the tensions inherent in the two roles.

Shaykh Ibrahim also includes the tarjama of his teacher and close relative, Shaykh Majid bin Khamis (d. 1928). Majid's early Qur'anic studies are mentioned in detail, as is his support for the nineteenth-century imamate of ʿAzzan ibn Qays (1868–71), during which he was appointed governor of the neighboring town of Bahla. This appointment involved him in organizing and directing tribal levies. Historical elements in Shaykh Majid's tarjama are interspersed with vignettes of personality and deeds—the construction of mosques, poetry, a list of scholars who studied under him, and his views on such topics as graveside Qur'anic readings, the sale of pious foundation land (*waqf*) to finance the imamate, innovations in almsgiving (*zakat*), and proper forms of prayer. The account at times verges on hagiography: Majid brought rain and reinvigorated the land wherever he went, divined water, healed a broken hand by touching it with the leaf from a tree in a region devoid of trees, and tamed a bull that had broken loose from its tether. Shaykh Ibrahim also records that "some say" that after Shaykh Majid's death there was a light and two green birds, "perhaps angels," over Shaykh Majid's grave (p. 182). Shaykh Majid's participation in the selection of the first two twentieth-century imams (1913 and 1920) is recorded, as is the blindness of his last years.

The other tarjamas incorporated into Shaykh Ibrahim's history contain many of the same elements, although they lack the hagiographic anecdotes. Ibadi tarjamas are more specifically grounded in political history than are their Moroccan counterparts, primarily because men of learning in Oman are closely identified with their tribes and, until the end of the imamate in 1955, acted politically on behalf of their tribes and the imam. And since the framework of political events is already known, Omani tarjamas focus on actions that favor the subject. Thus Shaykh Majid's tarjama recounts how in 1871, when he abandoned the cause of an imamate restoration just before its defeat, he opened the Qur'an and happened on a verse that indicated to him that God willed him and his retainers to slip out of the Bahla fortress at night rather than to remain to defend it against a more powerful enemy (p. 138). The action described is manifest, the motivation divinely inspired and not the result of individual choice.

Shaykh Ibrahim avoids certain topics—Saudi efforts to subvert the tribal leaders and ulama of the interior in the early

1950s, attitudes toward incorporation into the rule of the sultanate beginning in 1955, and the 1957 rebellion against sultanate rule. In a brief passage, Shaykh Ibrahim dryly writes that "hearts changed," and the Omani interior "all" went to the sultan: "There is no need for me to say what happened next" (p. 134). Indeed, if one is writing for an audience of contemporaries familiar with events and with what is *not* said, further elaboration is unnecessary.[18]

Conclusion

This essay shows the variation among Muslim societies in representing the lives of traditional men of learning. In spite of the common appeal to fixed and generalized elements, the representations in tarjamas differ according to social and political contexts and over time. Tarjamas are not a self-contained genre: they are intended for known audiences with access to additional, usually word-of-mouth, traditions complementing those of the tarjama.

It might be argued that there is a vast difference between the exemplars discussed here, drawn from the antipodes of the Arab Muslim world, and the persona of ulama contained, for example, in the biographical dictionaries of "classical" Islam, works that were intended presumably for a transregional network of men of learning. The tarjamas of such compendia should not be given a privileged position simply because their abstract and standardized nature make them appear more self-contained. They merely point to the persona sustained in contexts significantly different from those of nineteenth- and twentieth-century men of learning or, for that matter, those of other times and places in the "premodern" period.

Tarjamas select from the activities of learned individuals those elements that fit the prevailing cultural profile for men of learning. This process is a highly selective one, as only a limited number of individuals in Muslim societies can aspire to the persona of traditional men of learning. In the past, individuals could achieve full personhood on the basis of attributes other than learning, such as tribal leadership or royal authority, but full personhood is still confined to a limited number of individuals. In both Morocco and Oman, a distinction is made between "elite" (*nas khassa* or *ma'rufin*) and "commoners" (*al-'awam*), terms that distinguish between those who have reputations as men of learning and those who do not.

Until the late 1950s, a claim to family names going back multiple generations—one means of defining personhood and distinction from others—was confined to families of the elite and to learned persons. In Morocco, where religious roles were fluid, men of learning were sometimes considered to have saintly, or maraboutic, powers. Such powers could exist independent of religious knowledge. (The term *salih* [pious one] in Morocco can refer to a reputation based on various combinations of piety, learning, descent, mysticism, miraculous deeds, and maraboutic powers, and the weight given to these attributes has varied over time.) Thus in the 1930s, the Mansuri brothers found assistance in "discovering" their antecedents, but their preference was to emphasize the achieved status of learning over the ascribed one of descent. In 1919 the brothers' father was regarded locally as a *salih,* an attribute on which Ahmad Mansuri capitalized in arranging for the first French agricultural tax, collected in kind, to be delivered to his father's house. Tribespeople thought the tax was religiously sanctioned, and armed resistance to the French innovation was thereby avoided. Significantly, Ahmad's clever initiative is not recorded in his tarjama.

For the Mansuri brothers, as for Bu ʿAyyashi, distinguished descent is asserted but not explicitly demonstrated. Since their claims were widely recognized and unchallenged, there was no need to do so. The size of the community of men of learning in Morocco allowed considerable latitude for presenting and inventing such ties, but by and large, specific claims to descent, although still important, no longer carried the political and social privileges of earlier eras.[19] Bu ʿAyyashi's principal concern is to demonstrate his affinities with the nationalist movement,[20] and in doing so, he conveys the persona of the man of learning in the service of legitimate authority. For the Mansuri brothers, legitimate authority is the monarch. When the monarch acquiesced to French tutelage, so did the Mansuris; when the monarch opposed the French, so did they.

There is less latitude in Oman for expressing status and social location, for individuals are clearly located within specific frameworks of tribal identity. There is a greater expectation in Oman that a man of learning also be a man of action because of the closer links to tribal identity, in which the man of learning must balance his personas as one of the ulama and a responsible member of a tribal oligarchy. The latter identity, although not specifically Islamic, is implicit in the structure of the tarjama itself. One is expected to defend tribal interests, but in such a way as to advocate only those actions that can be justified in Islamic terms. Men of learning continue to show that their personas fulfill generalized, fixed principles, but the content of the principles and the choice of emphasis among them can vary considerably.

One remaining issue is how the self-representation of traditional men of learning is perceived by a younger generation, the product of an education different in form and emphasis from that of Qur'anic schools and mosque-universities and accessible to a much larger proportion of the school-age population. Modern education has broken the earlier ties between men of learning and the communities of which they were a part. In both Morocco and Oman, the older generation and many of the educated young share the expectation that political authority is legitimated or delegitimated in accord with divine law, although there is a difference of interpretation as to how this is done. The rulers of Morocco and Oman continue to regard the public expressions of legitimation from traditional men of learning as an important component of political legitimacy. Another legitimizing element is the rulers' ability to bring material progress and "development" to their subjects. For a younger generation, there is greater recognition of alternative interpreters of "what is Islamic" who are not legitimated by knowledge of a specific body of texts or by their predecessors. Indeed, the religious-minded can make such decisions for themselves.

The consequences for conceptions of self and person are as follows: In the past, few individuals could aspire to the persona of a man of learning, as expressed in tarjamas. Now the persona of the sincere, religious-minded believer has become more important and in some dimensions can recapture the early Islamic sense of personal responsibility mediated by only a few privileged interpreters of Islamic doctrine. Concepts of the *'alim* as a person are embedded in particular social contexts, and the way in which individuals achieve full personhood is much more open than in the past, including conceptions of religious knowledge not dependent on the forms exemplified in the tarjama. The persona of the tarjama is not so much attacked as displaced. As men of learning themselves possess qualities and attributes ranging beyond those signaled in tarjamas, many individuals take part in this quiet transformation of forms of valued religious knowledge and the social roles of their carriers.

3 Autobiography and Biography in the Middle East: A Plea for Psychopolitical Studies

Marvin Zonis

IN AN important article, Karl J. Weintraub distinguishes autobiography from memoirs, diaries, and other works by and about the self.

Autobiography adheres more closely to the true potential of
the genre the more its real subject matter is character, personality, self-conception—all those difficult-to-define matters which ultimately determine the inner coherence and meaning of life. Real autobiography is a weave in which self-consciousness is delicately threaded throughout interrelated experience. It may have such varied functions as self-explication, self-discovery, self-clarification, self-formation, self-presentation, self-justification. All these functions interpenetrate easily but all are centered upon an aware self aware of its relation to its experiences.[1]

Weintraub refers to the existence of an "autobiographic instinct" and urges the study of autobiography as the means best suited to revealing "the developing self-conceptions of Western men."[2] It is appropriate that he refers to "Western men" inasmuch as his examples are drawn entirely from the literature of Europe. Reviewing the output of such literature in the Arabic-, Persian-, and Turkish-speaking worlds, one would have to conclude that such an "instinct" is largely confined to Westerners and is not part of the constitution of those from the Middle East.[3] Those works from the region that achieve the "true potential of the genre" are few in number, limiting the utility of autobiography for illuminating Middle Eastern conceptions of the self.[4]

But not only is autobiography generally lacking; biographies, indigenous to the region, are also in relatively short supply.[5] The most obvious explanation for the paucity of these genres, even in the contemporary Middle East, appears to be that the concept of the individual human life as well as the "development" of that life over the course of the individual life cycle are profoundly different from such conceptions in the West.

Weintraub suggests why the genre of autobiography came to be common in the West:

It is the intent of this paper to argue the thesis that the autobiographic genre took on its full dimension and richness when Western Man acquired a thoroughly historical understanding of his existence. Autobiography assumes a significant cultural function around A.D. 1800. The growing significance of autobiography is thus a part of that great intellectual revolution marked by the emergence of the particular modern form of historical mindedness we call historism or historicism.[6]

That particular sensibility, Abdallah Laroui has made powerfully clear, has yet to grip the Middle East.[7] Historicism is the commitment to an understanding of a phenomenon as rooted in particular contexts that change over time with the result that the phenomenon itself may change. That commitment is not yet thoroughly subsumed within the culture of the Middle East. It is no wonder, then, that autobiography and biography are not yet part of the genres of literature in the Middle East. Both genres depend on the willingness to see a human life as a coherent whole with a history rooted in a variety of social, cultural, economic, and political contexts, where it is both possible and meaningful to assign, retrospectively, significance to the subject's life experiences and to the entire lived life. In the absence of a willingness and a capacity to understand a life in that way, the production of autobiography and biography will be limited. In their stead will be other related genres, such as memoirs, diaries, travelogues, and even lyrical poetry. These genres are similar to autobiography and biography in that they focus on the experiences of the author or subject. They differ in that they do not attempt an integration of those experiences to fashion an account of a lived life. Genres that focus on discrete lived experiences are common in the Middle East.

To be sure, more than one factor works against the production of autobiography and biography in the Middle East. Like all significant phenomena, the paucity of these genres is overdetermined. The absence of historicism is one contributing factor. But in addition, differential cultural emphases regarding the nature and meaning of the individual also reduce their incidence. It has been widely noted that concepts of the individual and individualism assume different dimensions in Middle Eastern and in Western cultures. Communal values are more widely cherished in the Middle East. The well-being of the community, even at the expense of the well-being of the individual (although there is certainly no necessary trade-off), is more highly valued in the Middle East than in the West. It could, in fact, be argued that if the three paramount values of Western society are liberty, equality, and fraternity, only fraternity is central to the value structure of the Middle East. The centrality of the value of community over individuality and individualism works against the production of both autobiography and biography, for that value lessens the need for the critical scrutiny of the individual life and the attempt to organize a life history into a coherent point of view and life pattern.

Thus both the absence of a sense of historicism and the relative underemphasis on the life of the individual in comparison with the group reduce the propensity for persons steeped in Middle Eastern culture to produce autobiographies and biographies. Not surprisingly, therefore, most such works written about the lives of Middle Easterners have been written by members of the intelligentsia who have been Westernized, most often those who have been educated in the West. Or, in many cases, they have been written by Westerners themselves.

The relative absence of autobiographies deprives investigators of the Middle East, both Western and Middle Eastern scholars, of the opportunity to examine first-person data on the life course as it is lived in the Middle East. In addition, the absence of autobiographies deprives investigators of insights into the shared principles by which individuals come to understand and make sense of their lives. This is because an autobiography is a retrospective reordering of one's life experiences on the basis of one's viewpoints and understandings held at the time of the reconstruction, not at the time of the lived experiences. As Weintraub suggests,

When the autobiographer has gained the firm vantage point from which the full retrospective view on life can be had, he imposes on the past the order of the present. The fact once in the making can now be seen together with the fact in its result. By this superimposition of the completed fact, the fact in the making acquires a meaning it did not possess before. The meaning of the past is intelligible and meaningful in terms of the present understanding; it is thus with all historical understanding.[8]

The value of autobiography as a source of insight into the nature of the lived life in the Middle East rests on the author's understanding of the past at the moment of authorship. Aside from completely idiosyncratic understandings of the past, the kind produced by those adjudged eccentric—geniuses or mad-persons—such understandings are part of the cultural repertoire of the author. They have been produced by that culture or been borrowed from other cultures, but they must be in the cultural repertoire of the author in order to be available for generating the understanding of the lived life. Thus, autobiography gives insights not only into how lives are lived but also into the organizing principles that inform the culture in which the autobiography is produced. Indeed, these two components are difficult to untangle.

But it is not only autobiography that provides investigators with insights into these phenomena. Biography is an equally rich source. Whether producing work about oneself or about another, the process elicits information about two central issues: the lived life and the principles for organizing an account of that life.

Insofar as these organizing principles are derived from Western culture, they will provide little insight into the ways in which Middle Easterners understand their own lives. This does not mean that Middle Easterners are better than Westerners at making sense of a life lived within a Middle Eastern culture. It is simply that Middle Eastern organizing principles can help us understand how Middle Easterners understand their own lives.

When that is not central to the investigation—and for most purposes I think it is largely irrelevant to the investigation—then there is no privileged status for either the autobiographer or the biographer from the Middle East. Western concepts can be as useful, if not more so, for assigning meaning and significance as concepts indigenous to the culture in which the life is lived.

Four recent extraordinary biographies of Middle Eastern figures have been produced, none by Middle Easterners.[9] They constitute the four most important biographies of modern Middle Eastern lives ever written. Fouad Ajami, Vincent Crapanzano, Roy Mottahedeh, and Vamik Volkan and Norman Itzkowitz, the authors of these works, came to their tasks with formidable credentials. All are deeply steeped in the cultures of the Middle East. They were born into Middle Eastern families or grew up in the region or had long residence there. In addition, three of the authors have had extensive psychoanalytic training, which has helped them to grasp the workings of the minds of their subjects and to produce sensitive yet powerful biographical treatments.

The four works seek to achieve somewhat different purposes: more or less political in focus, more or less interested in the psychological dimensions of their subjects, more or less attempting to learn of the intellectual, social, and political milieus in which their subjects were acculturated and which, in turn, were influenced by their subjects. But all four seek to "know the individuality of another," even if, as Crapanzano (quoting from Georg Simmel) reminds us, this knowledge is ultimately unobtainable.[10] Nevertheless, these studies are as successful in achieving that goal as any nonfiction work ever published about the lives of individuals from the Turkish, Arab, and Persian cultural worlds.

Two of the four works are explicitly nonpsychological. Mottahedeh strives to place his Shiʿite cleric within the context of contemporary Iranian culture and Shiʿite experience. In the sense that the author strives to say something of general significance about the place of Shiʿism in present-day Iran and the ways in which members of the Shiʿite intelligentsia come to terms with the world, the biography is more appropriately cultural and intellectual than psychological. Ajami's work on Musa al-Sadr can be understood in the same way. The story of the vanished imam is meant to do more than tell us of the life and death of a Shiʿite leader. It is also meant to account for the political power of Musa al-Sadr and the unusual links between him and his followers, which are at least partially explicable by the ways in which Musa al-Sadr embodied the principal myths of Shiʿism in his life and his disappearance. Ajami's work is also not psychological in any systematic sense.

The other two works are self-consciously psychological. Crapanzano attempts to present a psychological portrait of Tuhami through a flow of words that represent for his subject the "verbal objectification of the tension between 'reality' and desire structures by the author."[11] Volkan and Itzkowitz strive to present a psychological portrait of Atatürk that will allow the reader to gain access to his inner psychological processes and understand how his political actions spoke to his character structure.

Although all four studies—psychological or not—are successful as different types of biographies, they are less successful

in illuminating the political lives of their subjects. Of the four
works, *Tuhami* is the least committed to political investigation.
Yet the book contains fascinating insights into significant aspects of political power in Morocco. Crapanzano, through Tuhami, helps us understand the role of the king in Moroccan
society.[12] He also illuminates the nature of the power relationship between leader and follower by explicating the role of
dependency. He illustrates the crucial role of power and domination in interpersonal relationships, including those that are
not ostensibly political. He speaks, as well, of the ways in which
power is accumulated and preserved. Attributions of *baraka*
(divine grace), for example, are significant components of a
power base, but it is finally the doing of deeds that makes saints
powerful in the eyes of their devotees. Ironically, then, the biography that is the least oriented toward politics is rich with
insights for use by students of politics in the Middle East.

The remaining works, although explicitly oriented to politics, suffer to a greater or lesser degree from their failure to
focus on the intersection of psychological and political processes. As has already been noted, neither Ajami nor Mottahedeh take up the challenge of combining political with
psychological investigation. Only Volkan and Itzkowitz meet
that challenge. The basic narrative of the Volkan and Itzkowitz
psychobiography is a fascinating recounting of Atatürk's life,
with special attention to his brilliant successes as a military
leader and then as "Father Turk." Atatürk's life history is
chronicled in terms of conventional political explanations for
political acts, and the body of that narrative is devoid of psychological analysis. Only after the rich narrative history, in an
epilogue, is a compelling psychological portrait of Atatürk pre-

sented. Thus, the introduction of psychological variables to explain or provide rich accounts of Atatürk's significant political acts appears more an afterword than a central component of the analysis of the lived life.

This neglect of politics is not surprising given the central task of the psychobiographer. The thesis of this paper is that neither autobiography nor biography are useful genres for maximizing our generation of theories of the political process. As a type of biography, psychobiography suffers from the same shortcomings as its more abstract "parent." This paper argues that a particular kind of study, combining aspects of psychobiography and political analysis, can produce psychologically grounded understandings of important political events and thus contribute to the development of a body of theory that will come to constitute a specific academic discipline, that of psychopolitical studies.

Psychobiography is not useful in this goal of discipline building because the psychobiographical task is to "discern and assign meaning to a life" by employing psychological theories and modes of investigation.[13] The challenge and even the accomplishment of discerning and assigning meaning in order to fashion a coherent life account is different from the process of producing a psychopolitical study. In the latter effort, the emphasis must be placed on understanding the psychological underpinnings of particular political acts or events in which the subject was a participant, or of certain political ideologies or writings that were formulated or disseminated by the subject. The challenge is to understand the character structure of the person and the acts he or she committed, as well as the recip-

rocal relations between character and political behavior in so-
ciopolitical and interpersonal contexts.[14]

I have undertaken just such a study of the Iranian revolution.
Majestic Failure: The Fall of the Shah of Iran is a study of the
revolution from the point of view of the losers: the Shah and
the United States, his major foreign backer. The study focuses
on the Shah as the central actor of the revolution, that relatively
brief, year-long outpouring of rage, and attempts to explain
how he lost the revolution—a loss that resulted in his ouster,
the fall of the Pahlavi dynasty, and its replacement by the Islamic Republic led by the eighty-year-old Ayatollah Rouhollah
Khomeini.[15]

That the Shah lost the revolution is all the more remarkable
because of the resources he commanded. He had ruled his
country for thirty-seven years and presided over its transformation from a backward, isolated country to a prominent
regional power. The development of the oil industry had produced vast revenues that he had used to build the most powerful
armed forces in the Persian Gulf. The governmental bureaucra-
cies had also burgeoned, and the regime had undertaken vast
public projects as well as massive expansions of the educational
and social welfare systems. Iranian industry had blossomed, establishing a base for a powerful industrial sector.

In addition, the Shah could boast of support from all of the
major international states. The United States was his principal
champion, but the Soviet Union was not adverse to destroying
the Iranian Communist party to win his favor. The European
powers—East and West—counted themselves his supporters.
The last chief of state to pay an official visit to the Shah, in the

midst of the revolution, was the ruler of the People's Republic of China.

Yet despite his money, armed strength, and international diplomatic support, the Shah could not cope with the revolution. He failed to deal effectively with the complaints of his people and their demands for change. This study of the revolution suggests that a determining explanation for the failures of the Shah can be found in his character structure. It also suggests that his character and the actions that were consonant with that character were the most significant reasons for the rage that propelled the people of Iran into revolution.[16]

The Shah, it is argued, had emerged from his difficult childhood with a "narcissistic character structure." His youth, even after he was officially designated crown prince at the age of six, was no royal fairy tale. His mother was a powerful woman whose strength was exceeded only by that of her husband. When the young Mohammad Reza Shah was two, his father, Reza Shah, staged the coup that would eventually propel him and his son to the throne. Meanwhile, Reza Shah took another bride and was ostracized by his first wife, an unheard-of response in Iran in the 1920s. To take revenge on his first wife, Reza Shah later withdrew his eldest son from her care and installed him in a separate palace where he could be raised as a "man," free of her "feminizing" influences. After several years in his own palace, the crown prince was sent away again, to secondary school in Switzerland, also in the interests of preparing the boy for his future imperial responsibilities.

The Shah became an adult with depleted narcissism, with a level of self-esteem insufficient to maintain a reasonable psychic equilibrium. Instead, he was totally dependent for his narcissistic nurturing on external sources, of which he developed four.

One source was the Iranian people. He had a relationship with "his" people that led him to believe that he was genuinely respected and admired by them, if not loved. In short, he had come to believe his own press.

A second source feeding his self-esteem was his firm belief that he was protected by God. The Shah believed that he had been divinely chosen for his mission to lead the Iranian people to greatness. His belief stemmed from his early childhood when he recovered from three life-threatening illnesses and during each had visions of sacred figures from early Shiʿite-Islamic history. From that period on, he believed that he was protected by the Lord in order to fulfill his divine mission.

A third crucial source of psychic support came from certain intense personal relationships. The Shah derived strength from what, in effect, was a psychological merger with three other persons during different periods of his life. Through these "twinship" relations, the Shah was able to use the strength of others to aid his own functioning.

Finally, the Shah derived needed strength from his association with the United States. The Shah had met and worked with eight American presidents, from Franklin Delano Roosevelt, who first met the Shah when he came to Tehran to attend his wartime meetings with Churchill and Stalin, to Jimmy Carter, who came to Tehran and celebrated the Shah in his famous 1978 New Year's Eve toast. The American presidents became bastions of support for the Shah. He was restored to the throne through a CIA-sponsored coup in 1953 and received more than a billion dollars in aid through the remainder of the 1950s. But the peak of his relationship with the United States came with his designation by President Richard Nixon as America's virtual proxy in the Persian Gulf, after which the United States sold billions of dollars' worth of the most sophisticated American weapons to the Shah. The unusually close links between the two countries help explain the psychic dependency on the United States that the Shah developed.

As long as those sources of narcissistic supplies replenished him, the Shah could derive the self-esteem that he needed in order to "do" shah and not just to "be" shah. Beginning in the early 1970s, however, each of these sources of strength began to fail the monarch.

In February 1971, Iran experienced its first contemporary terrorist incident. A group of armed dissidents attacked a police post, killed many of its defenders, and withdrew into the neighboring forests surrounding the Caspian Sea. The terrorists were eventually captured, but their act initiated a series of attacks and killings and regime countermeasures that kept news of the armed enemies of the regime in the newspapers for the remainder of the decade.

Later in 1971, the Shah held the now infamous festivities in Persepolis to mark the 2,500th anniversary of the establishment of the monarchy in Iran. Heads of state and dignitaries from throughout the world attended the lavish spectacle, but few in Iran were invited. One result was to distance the Iranian people from the grandeur and pomp of the regime. Their dissatisfactions with the monarch became more obvious in the 1970s, dissatisfactions that the Shah found it increasingly difficult to ignore. With the outbreak of the revolution, he was devastated by the depth of the Iranian people's rejection of him.

The Shah's divine protection failed him as well when he learned in 1973 that he had cancer. He was told that the cancer, with proper attention, was not life threatening, but every day he had to take large numbers of pills, medication that reminded him of his illness and of his own mortality.

The Shah's third source of psychic support also failed him. He had established "twinship" relations with three others: Ernest Perron, Assadollah Alam, and his actual twin sister, Princess Ashraf Pahlavi. Ernest Perron, who was the son of the gardener at the Le Rosey School in Switzerland, had accompanied the Shah when he returned to Iran from his studies. Perron lived in one or another of the Shah's palaces until the mid-1950s, when he finally returned to Switzerland. His death in 1960 ended their intense mutual involvement. Following Perron's death, the Shah established or strengthened his "twinship" with Assadollah Alam. Alam served the Shah as prime minister and minister of court until he developed leukemia and died in November 1977. Just when the Shah needed Alam's strength to face the revolution—just when the Iranian people were about to demand the Shah's ouster—Alam died. Moreover, Alam died of cancer, fostering the Shah's belief that he had lost his own divine protection. Princess Ashraf, alive to this day and living in New York, was by then no substitute. She had become extremely unpopular with the people of Iran, and the Shah had gradually excluded her from his personal circle. She could play no useful role when he was most in need of her brilliantly calculating political judgment.

Finally, the Shah came to believe that he had lost his fourth source of narcissistic supplies. The 1976 nomination of Jimmy Carter as the Democratic candidate for United States President was greeted with grave concern in Tehran. Carter's campaign and inaugural address only exacerbated the panic in Iranian ruling circles, for Jimmy Carter demanded that United States foreign policy be reoriented. He sought two new emphases. He wanted the United States to insist on the realization of human rights throughout the world. And he wanted the United States to restrict the sale of weapons in order to diminish the international arms race and to tie the sale of those weapons to the institutionalization of human rights. The Shah understood Jimmy Carter to be talking first and foremost about Iran. He believed that President Carter was signaling a significant diminishing of the relationship between the United States and the Shah, a relationship that had been built throughout the terms of the previous seven American presidents.

As the dissatisfactions of the Iranian people turned to rage and as this rage was transformed into street demonstrations and then violence, the sources of psychological support that the Shah had been able to use in the past deserted him. He was thrown back on his own narcissistic resources, which were so inadequate that the Shah's psychological strength ebbed to the point where he could not act. He was effectively paralyzed.

In the face of this paralysis, the revolution grew, the rage of the Iranian people became more intense, and, in relatively short order, the Shah and his entire system were swept from the country. The revolution had completed its first phase, and Mohammad Reza Shah was its first victim. The revolutionaries had not so much won as the Shah had lost.

This is a summary of the argument made in the book *Majestic Failure*. The work attempts to provide a psychological explanation for the outbreak of the Iranian revolution and for the failure of the Shah to cope effectively with the demands of the revolutionaries and to suppress their attempts to oust him. This explanation is rooted in a psychoanalytic perspective that finds that significant childhood experiences of the Shah led to a particular narcissistic character structure. That character structure, in turn, meant that the Shah was unable to provide himself with sufficient psychic supplies—with enough of a sense of self-worth—to function effectively as the shah. Deprived of sufficient internal narcissistic supplies, the Shah turned to outside sources. As long as those sources, in his mind, provided him with the narcissistic supplies necessary to maintain his psychic equilibrium, the Shah could function, not always effectively, but usually with sufficient strength to rule. But as these sources of psychic strength failed him and he was unable to identify new sources, his narcissistic balance was shattered. He gradually became more depleted and less able to function. By the outbreak of the revolution, he was a broken man.

This exercise in psychopolitical studies is not a psychobiography, in that it is not concerned with the entire sweep of the shah's life, nor is its principal task to assign a coherent meaning to that life. It does provide significant amounts of biographical data in order to construct a character structure for the Shah that accounts for the observed qualities of the man during his life. But that is not the purpose of the investigation. It creates a character structure that makes sense of his life, but it does not stop there and for this reason, as well, fails to qualify as a psychobiography. Rather, the study proceeds to a third phase, an examination of a particular political phenomenon, in this case, the revolution of 1978–79. The Shah was a single political actor with immense potential power vis-à-vis that political event. By focusing on his behavior and how that behavior emanated from his character structure, the study uses psychological variables to explain a set of political processes.

This investigation of the Iranian revolution is an example of the genre of social scientific research here called psychopolitical studies. The outcome of the Iranian revolution was determined by the actions and inactions of the Shah of Iran in the face of the mounting rage of the Iranian people. Those actions in turn were consequences of the Shah's particular character structure, whose functioning had altered over the course of his rule through his social and political relations with others and, as the Shah believed, with the Lord.

Psychopolitical studies differ from psychobiography because the former focuses on political processes and uses psychology to explain those processes. The goal of such studies is not to make a lived life coherent by assigning meaning but to explain the nature and outcome of political phenomena.

Psychopolitical studies, then, will be concerned with the explanation of political phenomena, but not with their prediction. If social scientists are to improve the quality of their investigations, they must abandon prediction as a significant enterprise, at least in terms of predicting the outcome of complex political events. Social scientists with long experience in the Middle East frequently make successful predictions about complicated political phenomena; so do diplomats and professional politicians. Successful prediction is a particular kind of achievement, hardly restricted to the social sciences, that suggests a familiarity with "what follows what" or "what goes with what" or the "association among variables." But to make predictions through the construction of a series of interrelated and meaningful theoretical propositions is a more difficult task, one requiring the identification of the relevant variables, an understanding of those variables, and a comprehensible explanation for their relationships.

Furthermore, most variables of interest to the social scientist relate through a human agency: the dependent variable is affected by the independent variable because intervening between the two are the mental processes of human actors. Take, for example, the area of voting studies, an area of social science investigation in which prediction has been impressively accurate, if not particularly profound. In most voting studies, people are asked to give their voting preferences and intentions; it is not surprising that a high correlation exists between these expressions of intention and subsequent behaviors. Other voting studies attempt to link social variables—economic conditions, political repression, strategic power, international relations, and the like—to voting behavior. These variables are often highly associated with voting behavior, but understanding why the variables relate to each other as they do entails the application of psychology, the study of human mental processes. Intervening between economic conditions, for example, and the act of voting or political protest or any other dependent variable of social scientific interest is the human agency, with its mental processes and character structure. To understand fully the relationship between the independent and dependent variables, one must understand the way the human "black box," intervening between the other variables, serves to link the two. Thus psychology lies at the heart of the concept of social science explanation.

To expect to link the variables, however, in a predictive fashion is another matter. The prediction of complicated socio-political phenomena through the construction of sophisticated models whose operations are not merely empirically known but also theoretically explicable and, therefore, sensible is still beyond the capacity of the social sciences. For the foreseeable future—indeed, perhaps indefinitely—the construction of such models will be possible only for phenomena of scant interest to the social sciences.[17]

This is not the case, however, for postdiction. Social science theories can be developed most effectively through retrospective examination. The historical examination of events or processes allows for the identification of variables as significant components of the particular process. The examination of those components in other historical processes is one form in which the model that has been produced can be "tested." In short, it appears possible to explain in the social sciences, but not necessarily to predict.

This act of retrospective explaining is best done through a case study. William Runyan suggests that "a case study is undertaken in response to a problem in understanding."[18] The social sciences and their individual disciplines and subdisciplines would appear to be reflections of widespread problems in understanding. The case study is not the only possible response to such problems; yet case studies must be a central component of psychopolitical studies and will be a more useful part of such studies than will psychobiographies, or treatments of an entire life. Runyan presents two separate definitions of the case study. First, he suggests that "a case study may be defined as the systematic presentation of information about the life of a single unit." Then, he suggests that "a case study may be defined as 'a reconstruction and interpretation' based on the best evidence available, of part of the story of a person's life."[19]

Hans-Georg Gadamer argues more forcefully for the case study:

Surely we can admit that all historical knowledge involves the application of general empirical regularities to the concrete problems it faces; yet, the true intention of historical knowledge is not to explain a concrete phenomenon as a particular case of a general rule. . . . In actuality, its true goal—even in utilizing general knowledge—is to understand an historical phenomenon in its singularity, in its uniqueness. Historical consciousness is interested in knowing not how men, people, or states develop *in general,* but, quite on the contrary, how *this* man, *this* people, or *this* state became what it is; how each of these *particulars* could come to pass and end up specifically *there.*[20]

But psychopolitical studies, although based on the study of particular cases, should not necessarily be restricted to the study of the individual political actor. Insofar as such studies are restricted, they are related to and bear a family resemblance to psychobiography. But in addition, psychopolitical studies must concern themselves with the study of group phenomena, of which several variations exist. One kind of group phenomena is found when many individuals are responsible for a single political decision or act, as, for example, in collective leadership or collective political action. The United States decision to supply arms to Iran, now known as the Iran-Contra Affair, appears to be a classic example of a decision that was reached by a number of political actors for various political and personal reasons.

The president of the United States appears to have sought the link as a way to free the Americans held captive in Lebanon and thus to spare himself the anguish resulting from his own inability to rescue them. That anguish appears to have been a blend of his deep personal commitment to alleviate human suffering and his capacity to best understand the nature of such suffering on a personal basis, on the level of individual human beings rather than abstract phenomena such as whole groups or nations. His anguish was also bred of the pleas that had been made directly to him by the parents, spouses, and children of the hostages. Finally, it appears also to have stemmed from his eagerness to avoid being compared to his predecessor, President Jimmy Carter, who was unable to free the United States diplomats held captive by the Iranians for 444 days.

There certainly were other key actors. The CIA director appears to have been primarily concerned with the fate of William Buckley, the CIA station chief in Beirut, who had been seized by the Islamic Jihad. Director William J. Casey was concerned about the suffering Buckley would likely undergo at the hands of his captors and also about the secrets Buckley knew that would damage American intelligence in the Middle East were he tortured and forced to talk, as the CIA believed would inevitably be the case. Furthermore, Casey still smarted from the losses that the agency had suffered in Beirut during his directorship. Robert Ames, the National Intelligence officer for the Middle East, and the entire staff of the Beirut CIA station were killed when a terrorist bomb destroyed the United States Embassy in April 1983. Casey sought to protect his agents in the field, to maintain the morale of his employees, and to preserve the intelligence capabilities of the United States.

There were yet other actors with other commitments in the decision to supply weapons to the Iranians. The CIA had generated a report in early 1985 arguing that some officials within the ruling clergy of the Islamic Republic of Iran were interested in contacts with the United States. These contacts were seen as potentially useful for the strategic position of the United States and for moderating Iranian support for terrorism, its commitment to export the Islamic revolution, and its pursuit of the war with Iraq. It appears that some American officials who urged the decision to supply weapons to Iran were interested in altering that country's foreign policy, if not its domestic politics as well.

Other officials, first in the CIA and then elsewhere, feared mounting Soviet influence in Iran and even the possibility of a Soviet military thrust into Iran as a way of aiding Soviet proxies. These American officials believed that supplying American weapons to the Iranian regime would accomplish at least two relevant goals: The arms would send a signal to the Soviets that the United States still maintained a commitment to the territorial integrity and independence of Iran. The arms would also strengthen the Iranian military against a possible Soviet invasion.

Other officials in the National Security Council saw the sale of arms to Iran as a means to bail the Nicaraguan Contras out of their increasingly dire financial and political straits. With the refusal of the United States Congress to supply weapons or financial assistance to the Contras, their cause had nearly collapsed. Profits from the sale of weapons to Iran could be channeled to the Contras to reverse their fortunes. If the Reagan administration later succeeded in changing Congressional opposition to additional funding for the Nicaraguan "freedom fighters," the arms supply to Iran could be ended.

This abbreviated account of the motives and goals that underpinned the Iran-Contra Affair has dealt only with the American actors. There were foreign actors as well. Israeli officials had their own reasons for supplying weapons to Iran and also for urging the United States to do so. In addition, certain arms dealers had private, financial motives for working toward the opening of a military supply relationship between the United States and Iran.

The point of this discussion is to indicate that in many political situations a focus on the role of a single actor presents an impoverished view of the political event. Even when the focus of the inquiry is narrow—the United States decision to supply weapons to Islamic Iran—it is necessary to examine more than one actor and more than one "motive" of any given actor to understand, in its complex richness, the basis of even a simple decision. This is especially true when the decision is not simple and when there is not a clear chain of command with an officially designated and universally accepted decision maker.

In addition to the study of group decision making, other group phenomena are important for future psychopolitical studies. Interactions among actors also produce politically significant results. Such is clearly the case when one is studying the behaviors of crowds or mobs. But group phenomena are present outside the study of the political behaviors of "the masses." Terrorism, for example, has been explained as the result of a complex series of relationships among certain kinds of members of an intelligentsia.[21] Similarly, insofar as political decisions are the result of group processes, an exclusive focus on the minds of individual decision makers will miss the consequences of group dynamics for political decisions.[22] It is the case, therefore, that psychopolitical studies must not be limited to the study of individual political actors but must also consider group phenomena as well.

Irrespective of whether psychopolitical studies focus on the postdictive interpretation and explanation of individual or of group processes, such studies confront a problem of validity that is profound and troubling. For the time being, it is difficult to imagine a satisfactory solution to the challenges that bedevil the question of validity in psychopolitical studies. By validity, we refer to the problem of assessing the legitimacy or appropriateness of an interpretation or, as Vincent Crapanzano has put it, of understanding that the real is a metaphor for the truth and distinguishing the latter from the former.[23] How does the investigator of a psychopolitical phenomenon know when a particular understanding of a phenomenon is valid, and how does a reader of that scholarship come to accept the legitimacy of that interpretation?

There is a common solution to the problem of validity, which approximates the solution to the problem of validity advanced in other sciences. As Runyan suggests, the problem of validity can be solved through the judgments of people who are familiar either with the subject of the psychobiographical investigation or with other sources of information about the subject.[24] Ultimately, the problem of validity must be solved by the consensual opinion of others. There is no so-called objective way to establish "truth" in psychobiographical and, by extension, psychopolitical investigation. Validity, in short, is consensual validity.

This should be far from a cause for despair. Rather than leading either proponents or critics of psychopolitical studies to question the scientific status of the enterprise, it would be more appropriate to recognize the central status of consensual validation in virtually all scientific endeavors, or, indeed, perhaps in all communication. Peter Winch refers to "discourse universes," and E. D. Hirsch stresses the significance of language and communication since "the process of understanding is itself a process of validation."[25]

The so-called hard sciences may have developed instrumentation to calibrate and replicate their findings, but those instruments are useful for validation because scientists accepted as knowledgeable have agreed that the instruments measure what the scientists claim. In short, the disciplines of the academic world constitute communities of investigators who share expertise about particular phenomena and ways of investigating those phenomena that are, in the minds of the members of those disciplines, appropriate.[26]

The challenge confronting the practitioners of psychopolitical studies is not whether there ought to be a separate or different method of validation for these studies than for those of other disciplines. There is no reason to expect or demand a different set of procedures for determining validity in psychopolitical studies than in any other field of inquiry that purports to be scientific in the Western sense of that term.

The problem with validity in psychopolitical studies is rather that the size of the community who could legitimately pass on the validity of a given interpretation may be so narrow as to be limited to the individual investigator. There are two reasons for this. First, the number of practitioners of systematic psychopolitical studies is extraordinarily small, and second, the "discipline" of psychopolitical studies does not exist in any effective fashion.

Psychopolitical studies are not in a "preparadigmatic" state but rather have a variety of competing paradigms in both components of the enterprise—the investigation of political and of psychological processes—none of these paradigms having managed to assert their intellectual dominance. Moreover, there is no reason to believe that there will ever be a single paradigm in the study of either politics or psychology that will compel, by its intellectual power, the loyalty of a significant majority of the practitioners of psychopolitical studies.

Psychoanalysis, for example, is the single most widely used foundation of psychopolitical studies, but psychoanalysis, in its present manifestation, is itself far from a unified paradigm. There have been three stages in the articulation of the discipline; theories and methods from each stage remain important to the present. The field is clearly dominated by the works of its creator, Sigmund Freud. His basic clinical methods as well as the intellectual grounding of many of his central theories remain widely accepted to this day. But even during his lifetime, many who had originally been his disciples turned away to develop significant modifications of their own. Both Adler and Jung, for example, created alternative theoretical formulations that are used by present-day psychopolitical investigators. The second stage of psychoanalysis began shortly after Freud's death. Significant modifications in his work were then created by those who considered themselves solidly within the intellectual legacy of the master. For example, the ego was assigned a more substantial position in the operation of the psyche than was the case in Freud's writings. The third stage began more recently as the works of Heinz Kohut have dramatically altered Freud's legacy yet have left Kohut and his followers within psychoanalysis.

Thus psychoanalysis is far from a unified discipline. Psychopolitical investigators who apply a psychoanalytic approach to their research will differ dramatically in the kinds of work they do, the kinds of questions they pursue, the kinds of data they consider meaningful, and the kinds of interpretations they make. As Roy Schafer has suggested, "There is no single, necessary, definitive account of a life history. . . . What have been presented as the plain empirical data and techniques of psychoanalysis are inseparable from the investigator's precritical and interrelated assumptions concerning the origins, coherence, totality, and intelligibility of personal action."[27] Those "assumptions" arise from within psychoanalysis itself as well as from other theoretical frameworks and from broader cultural beliefs and practices.

But outside of psychoanalysis, an even larger number of psychological approaches to the study of political phenomena may be found. There are what may be thought of as subdisciplines within psychopolitical studies, defined by the common commitments of their members to shared theories and methods. As a result, there will be many intellectual communities whose members can agree on the validity of particular interpretations because they share the commitments of the interpreter. But there is little likelihood that agreement will be produced between subdisciplines, those mini-intellectual communities whose dogged commitment to their particular approaches was described by Freud as the "narcissism of small differences."

The validity problem in psychopolitical studies is exacerbated because of the difficulty of communicating all the nuances of data and meaning that led to the interpretation at issue. No one knows the subject under investigation as deeply as the investigator, who has a privileged status vis-à-vis the subject since he or she has been immersed in and has developed a feel for the subject that is extraordinarily difficult to convey. Even Freud, that great prose master, had difficulty communicating the richness of his interpretations and the nuances of his data, although he did it better than anyone else.

Given all this, the communities from which judgments of validity will emanate will be small in size. There will be significant disagreements, even from within what appears to be the same paradigm, because the number of "validation communities" will be substantial. As a consequence, the practitioners of a scientific enterprise will have to tolerate extraordinarily broad criteria for validity or witness an even greater fragmentation of psychologically based studies of political processes. That does not mean that there are no validity criteria at all, that any interpretation is as good as any other. Within the subdisciplines of the field, the criteria for validity will be explicit, if not always easily applicable. Across fields there will still be common commitments to more overarching modes of intellectual inquiry. Yet ultimately, there are no simple and universal validity criteria.

In our efforts as critical readers, our first task must be to try to adopt the subdisciplinary framework of the author—as long

as the subdiscipline falls within the tolerant limits of the field
and seeks validity within the paradigms on which that work is
based. If it does not, then we are not dealing with a science,
and conventional intellectual approaches to the question of validity are irrelevant.

But if the subdiscipline does fall within conventional definitions, then it is necessary to work within that subdiscipline to
determine validity, not an easy thing to do. Few of us are trained
across subdisciplinary boundaries. Even fewer can lay claim to
the intellectual eclecticism necessary to work effectively across
such boundaries or the intellectual tolerance to do so. Moreover, we shall never be able to capture the subject as effectively
as the investigator, given his or her lengthy immersion in the
research.

Validity, in short, is a nearly insolvable issue. We should never
cease to search for it or for more adequate ways to determine
it, but we need to operate in a tolerant intellectual framework
and be willing to function with validity criteria less certain than
most of us would conventionally deem essential. In the process,
we need to accept conclusions that are "conditioned and in-
complete" as well as tentative and uncertain.[28] Lack of certain
conviction, however, has never been an impediment to scientific
inquiry. To the contrary, it is the impetus for scholarly investigation.

Through the tentative conclusions of psychopolitical studies—the use of psychology to investigate political phenomena—we are most likely to produce an understanding of those
processes and so begin to generate theories applicable to other
phenomena at other times and in other places.

4 Biography and Psychohistory

Elie Kedourie

WE MAY look on biography as a species of historical investigation. It is the attempt to give an account of a subject's thoughts and actions in the context of his or her own time and place. But a question arises: why should anyone think it useful or interesting to embark on such an investigation? The question is all the more natural since biography is not a universal genre to be found everywhere or at all times. To take a case in point, in the domain of traditional Islam, biography as briefly described here is unknown. There are of course biographical dictionaries of ulama, the traditionists and learned men; here and there in the literature may be found brief accounts of governors and rulers. All of these provide no more than brief and stylized details about those aspects of the subjects' lives that are, in terms of the self-view that is associated with the world of Islam, considered the most important and the most worthy of notice. Traditional Islamic literature has no equivalent of *Plutarch's Lives,* or Thomas More's biography of his son-in-law, or Monypenny and Buckle's *Life of Disraeli.* Even more striking is the utter absence not only of women's biographies but also of even the scantiest detail about the mothers, wives, or daughters of those men who are the subject of biographical notices. There are, of course, good reasons why such detail was considered inappropriate, but this absence is significant in itself as a pointer to a lack of interest, within traditional Muslim culture, in individuals as individuals, with their own specific characteristics and peculiar quirks. Men are seen as belonging to well-established categories, and the particular category is deemed to indicate how a person who belongs to it behaves: Muslim or non-Muslim, ⁽alim or vizier, military commander or ruler. Biography as an exercise in understanding another human being as fully as possible, and understanding this person simply for the sake of understanding, seems to be a modern Western notion—an invention that has its roots in Western culture but has characteristics that have been articulated and theorized within, say, the last hundred years.

History, then—of which biography is a branch—is a genuinely new enterprise. It is commonly said that Islam is historically minded, and as the Bible shows, the same may be said of Judaism as well as of Christianity; the latter is, or has been, said to be a historical religion. How are we to understand such statements? What they mean is that at one point in the past a divine revelation or a divine intervention took place that is the beginning of what may be called a sacred history. All that follows is the working-out of the consequences of this divine intervention, and the consequences of obeying or, as the case may be, disobeying divine injunctions. History here is a guide to believers, a repository of stories and rules of behavior that will enable them to lead lives pleasing in the eyes of God. This sacred history, then, is a kind of practical history, making use of the past in order to engage in the successful practice of living here and now. There are other kinds of practical history, the most prevalent, and the most efficient, being the history that serves to instill a sense of pride or glory in the body politic. Other kinds of history may serve as a storehouse of precedents, legal or administrative, or may be used to defend a particular religion or political cause, or are designed to teach political prudence.

However, this practical attitude to the past is not history as history came to be invented or discovered—a term used advisedly, for this attitude is indeed a new discovery made by Westerners about themselves and their past, a new invention dealing in a new way with the fact that people have succeeded one another through the generations and successively left layer on layer of fragments that can be read as evidence of past thought and past activity.

This new discovery or invention has been called *Historismus* by the German philosophers and historians who have been prominent in articulating and theorizing it. The English equivalent, as adopted by the translator of Friedrich Meinecke's book on the development of *Historismus,* is historism. This term is distinct from, and signifies something very different from, what is commonly known as historicism. Historicism, it is well known, as anathematized by Karl Popper and his many followers, is the belief that there exists a pattern that governs human history and that unfolds with an irresistible inevitability. Whether the pattern is cyclical as in Plato, or linear as in Augustine or Bossuet, historicism is at the opposite pole from historism.

There are three other views, in addition to historicism, that are very influential but quite incompatible with a properly historical view of the past. The first is that human existence is a manifestation over time of our unchanging essence, the second is that people's actions are exemplifications of unchanging eternal laws, and the third is that there is an underlying structure in human nature or in society that governs all visible action or thought that may be called superstructure. Marxism is today the most influential, but by no means the only, variant of such a belief.

The properly historical view may be summed up by saying that man's nature is his history. This view signifies that there is nothing beyond or above or below the historical record (as the evidence shows it to be) that may serve to account for or to explain this record, that the record is, in short, its own explanation, that a subject, to quote Hegel, is the series of his or her actions. In such a record, there is nothing extraordinary (to borrow a word that occurred in the original title of this conference) because there is nothing ordinary either. The pair of ideas, ordinary–extraordinary, imply a norm of human behavior to which people conform or from which they depart. But given that people are mind and will, and that, as such, their actions cannot be programmed or predicted, then it follows that there are no norms against which human actions or thoughts can be judged. Extraordinary lives are legendary lives, and the historian's work is to make legend explicable in terms of human actions and responses.

The historian's work is possible because mind speaks to mind or, as sometimes put, because of the "I" that is in the "thou." This does not mean that the historian possesses magical powers that open up the minds of others for exploration. Rather, the historian is able to write history because minds have objectified themselves in utterances, artifacts, and institutions that are open to inspection and that one may aspire to understand because they are the expressions of minds with which

one's own mind is kin: mind speaks to mind. For if these utterances and performances are not the expressions of human
minds, then they are and must remain hopelessly unintelligible
to the historian. But again and again we do find that they are
intelligible: Champollion deciphers the Rosetta stone, Goldziher disentangles the confusion of *hadith,* Prescott penetrates
the secrets of the Aztecs, Mommsen probes the intricacies of
Roman administration, and Syme explores late Republican politics. It can be done—and is done every day—in spite of the fact
that Champollion is not the nephew of a Pharaoh, nor is the
Orientalist Goldziher an Oriental, Prescott a descendant of Aztecs, or Mommsen and Syme survivals from the time of Augustus and Cicero.

The philosopher Dilthey, who more than anyone else strove
to establish the main lines of what he called a critique of historical reason, held that because the object of history is a mind-
affected world, then it is biography that is the best entrance into
history. Whether one agrees with him or not, biography, in this
view, is the attempt to make intelligible the thought and action
originating in a particular mind over the whole course of its
life. History is the asking of questions from the evidence. The
questions that are asked arise from the evidence, but they are
not themselves to be found in the evidence. Evidence is itself
inert and lifeless until a particular mind with all its ingenuity
and originality comes to recognize it as evidence and, so to
speak, to vivify it. It is therefore utterly misleading to imagine
that history, seen in this way, is an assemblage of "facts" or
"materials," or that historians are mere collectors of "facts"
that they only put together, as a child puts together the pieces
of a prearranged puzzle.

If history begins with the asking of questions, then the notion of total history, made fashionable by Braudel and the school of the *Annales,* is misconceived. A historian begins by asking a question because something in the evidence or the account being examined is obscure and puzzling. One question leads to another, until the particular puzzlement that led to the initial inquiry is, as far as possible, banished. Then comes another historian, with a different set of puzzlements and a different set of questions, and so on ad infinitum. This is why it is commonly, and rightly, said that every generation writes its own history. One may go further and say that, since no historian's mind is identical with that of any other historian, every historian writes a unique history: there are no standard histories, no so-called authorities. Similarly, there can be no given quantum or totality that one can hope to cover, and once you have covered it, you have produced total history. Take any subject and survey the literature about it, and you may easily see how revolution follows on revolution in this field: the life of the Prophet from Ibn Hisham to Montgomery Watt to Suleyman Bashir, the Abbasid "revolution" between M. A. Sha'ban and Moshe Sharon, and Afghani from Edward G. Browne's and C. C. Adams's wide-eyed pieties to a book whose subtitle proclaims its subject's religious unbelief and his political activism.

Biography, then, like history, is the asking of questions the answer to which makes intelligible, for instance, the passage of Disraeli from the dissipated dandy of the 1830s to the prime minister of the 1870s, or the passage of Nuri b. Sa'id from the small conspiratorial lieutenant of 1914 into the prime minister of the Arab Federation over whose mutilated corpse the Baghdad mob danced with glee in 1958. In all these biographies, there is nothing expected or normal or ordinary, and yet nothing that is rebellious to historical discourse. The passage in question here is a passage over time, and the substance of it is made up of actions and responses for which evidence exists; of that for which no evidence exists, thereof one must be silent.

For evidence, there is no substitute. Some speak of a so-called conceptual history, with concepts serving as some kind of scaffolding or framework holding together the bricks of historical "facts," which in turn serve to make the conceptual skeleton attractive with color and decoration. But some such metaphor cannot help being misleading since a historical account is not made up of concepts plus "facts"; it is wholly made up of pieces of evidence interlocking with other similar pieces without, so to speak, being forced. And if there is no evidence, then no concept can make up for its absence. An economic, social, or psychological theory cannot substitute for evidence. The temptation, however, to make use of such a short-cut—a temptation that Carlo Antoni has examined and illustrated in his book *From History to Sociology*[1]—is, considering the flourishing condition of the social sciences in the academy, one that must be very difficult to withstand.

It may, however, be said that action is the expression of personality, and that to understand the action we must understand the personality. This is to speak as though the personality is the cause and action the effect: male babies are mother-fixated whereas female children suffer from penis jealousy, therefore—therefore what? This kind of explanation, whether Freudian or Adlerian or Jungian or Pavlovian or other, is at the basis of psychobiography and more generally psychohistory. The "psycho" in psychohistory is a reference to the science of psychology, a science that deals with unconscious drives and involuntary impulses or reactions, that seeks to explain them and to explain how thoughts and actions are "conditioned" by them. The science is a chain of hypothetical reasonings that, as in all sciences, take the form, if—then. Like all sciences, it is subject to continuous contention and revision and cannot, therefore, be the sturdy structure on which to base history.

Psychobiography proves too little: you cannot establish an evidential chain from an Oedipus complex to a decision to bomb Tripoli. It also proves too much: every Oedipus complex must lead to warlike proclivities. Psychobiography, again, must assume that behind all actions there are hidden motives, unknown to the agent. If so, this must be equally true of the psychobiographer. We then should not ask, for example, whether what the psychobiographer says of James V. Forrestal's psychosis is true, but rather what drives he seeks to satisfy, or what unconscious motives lead him, when he is making such statements about the United States defense secretary. We then find ourselves revolving in a vicious circle: in this cabinet of Dr. Caligari, it can never be established who is mad, the biographer or his subject.

5 A Response to Critics of a Psychobiography

Vamik D. Volkan and Norman Itzkowitz

 MUSTAFA Kemal Atatürk, born in 1881, was the founder of modern Turkey. After World War I, in which the Turks fought against the Allies, the Ottoman Empire collapsed, and Turkey was invaded. The Turks generally believe it was Atatürk who, almost single-handedly, inspired his war-weary compatriots to fight a war of independence. A brilliant military man, he became the first president of the modern Turkish nation and instituted drastic cultural changes that did much to westernize it. Although he died in 1938, he is venerated in Turkey much as though he were still alive. His representation as "The Eternal Leader" is immortalized.

In 1984 the University of Chicago Press published his psychobiography, *The Immortal Atatürk*. It was written from an unabashedly psychoanalytic perspective by a psychoanalyst and a historian.[1] Since the book's publication, it has received more attention from both scholars and lay persons than had been anticipated, and it has been reviewed in journals of different disciplines—psychoanalysis, history, political science, and political psychology—and in magazines and newspapers in the United States, Turkey, England, Israel, and northern Cyprus. In these reviews, and in the Tel Aviv conference on biography, the Atatürk psychobiography was praised. But criticism was of-

97

fered as well, and doubts were expressed as to the value of applying psychoanalytic concepts to the understanding of leaders, especially those of the Middle East. This chapter does not discuss the methodology of psychoanalytic biography,[2] nor repeat our findings on Atatürk. It will deal directly with criticisms raised by our work, the first of which was the claim that the psychoanalytic approach to biography is of little value, and reductionist at best.

In addressing this claim, we concluded that our critics had leapt to the conclusion that all psychobiography is written from the standpoint of Freudian beliefs, for which these critics had little tolerance. We suspected that those taking this view would dismiss Marxist historiography, women's studies, or quantitative historiography—indeed, anything new, largely because it is new, without asking why they find such enterprises threatening. In particular, they see something pruriently sexual in psychoanalysis, ignoring its use as a comprehensive model of the human mind and a key to understanding the intricacies of how we consciously and unconsciously see our world and balance internal against external demands. One Turkish reviewer remarked that reading our psychobiography of Atatürk was like entering his bedroom, a shocking performance for a Turk; this comment suggests that Atatürk represented the oedipal father to him. A few reviewers made fun of our psychoanalytic interpretations, and we felt this reaction might point to an effort by them to reverse anxiety that had been aroused by the sexual formulations. We were challenged, for example, on our explanation of Atatürk's refusal, or inability, to visit the former Ottoman capital of Istanbul after it became politically possible. He left that city for Anatolia in May 1919 to open the Turkish struggle for independence, a struggle that ended in October 1922. The visit he made to Istanbul in July 1927 was his first since leaving in 1919. We know that in the interim he was preoccupied with making the little Anatolian town, Ankara, into the capital of the new Turkey, but he could have gone to Istanbul during this time. We ascribed psychological reasons, both conscious and unconscious, for his not doing so, and he confirmed our intuitions about this in his own words, as we made clear in our book. It was his own utterance that explained how Istanbul had become a symbol for him. William Niederland has written of how a geophysical entity can represent externalized images, wishes, and fears.[3] The ability to symbolize differentiates humans from animals, but apparently our critics were unwilling to conceive of how Istanbul represented to the Turkish leader at this particular time in his life a mother to whom he was ambivalently related, possibly because this seemed to them an uncalled-for sexual reference.

Some of the criticisms have been so far off the mark that one is obliged to conclude that the critic either failed to read the whole book or was unable to understand the work. It seems obvious that the reviewers approached the book from long-held positions that they felt obliged to defend, and they failed to judge the material on its own merits.

To respond further to such critics would be to belabor the unending and largely intellectualized arguments heard since the days of Freud as to whether psychoanalysis is a science, and whether it is prurient. Peter Gay in his recent work on the life and times of Freud indicates that since Freud's proclamation of a dynamic unconscious and psychic determinism, psychoanalysis has been a favorite target for the wrath of certain intellectuals and pseudointellectuals.[4] We are reminded of Freud's musing that the discovery that the world is not the center of the universe, and then the claims of evolutionary theory, dealt narcissistic blows to humanity; clearly, the conclusion that a person has a dynamic unconscious, that the mind operates according to certain patterns, and that we are not always rational tops off the list of such injuries, injuries to which some of our critics appear to react still. In the words of Matthew Arnold,

> Let the long contention cease!
> Geese are swans, and swans are geese.
> Let them have it how they will
> Thou art tired, best be still.

Reviewers who gave our work serious consideration usually agreed with some of our formulations, but the comments of some demand a response. First, it seems curious that these reviews appeared in journals for those interested in psychoanalysis or for historians or specialists in Near Eastern studies— and that the reviewers were specialists in one of these fields, without any real knowledge of the other. The writing of the Atatürk psychobiography was a collaboration between a historian with psychoanalytic training and a clinical psychoanalyst with a long-held interest in political psychology and familiarity from birth with the Turkish culture. The joint effort pooled diverse resources in such a way as to enhance the skills of each and to preclude any ill-founded conclusions. But few of the reviewers were capable of crossing over from psychoanalysis to history, or vice versa. In general, the reviews in psychoanalytic journals accepted the psychoanalytic conclusions (in spite of some remarks indicative of the operation of Freud's "narcissism of minor differences") but criticized some aspects of the historical analysis, the writer of one psychoanalytic journal praising our representation of psychoanalytic concepts but pointing to "historical flaws." At the same time, specialists in history took a more favorable view of historical aspects of the book than of the analytic material.

Second, although we took pains to make it clear that even the Armenians do not accuse Kemal Atatürk of being involved in the Armenian deportation, massacres, and countermassacres, much review space was unprofitably devoted to the Armenian issue. This matter is one much before the public today, and we sincerely hope that Armenians and Turks will make peace, sort out reality from emotional misperceptions, acknowledge each other's grief, and validate each other's humanity and self-esteem. But such matters lie beyond the scope of our book, in which our aim was to map out Atatürk's mind, a mind that did not harbor genocidal thoughts toward any ethnic group.

Freud was keenly aware that "biographers are fixated on their heroes in a quite special way."[5] He noted that a subject was often chosen on the basis of some special regard that arose from the writer's own emotional life, and he feared that the result might be biased accordingly. We noted Freud's comments about the idealization of the hero but recognized that devaluation of a public figure may also be the motivation for a biographer when the subject has become a displacement figure on which hatreds generated in the writer's own childhood have been placed. We suggest that reviewers may also have transference feelings about the subject of a biography; under some circumstances, leaders, ethnicity, and nationality evoke strong and raw emotions that color perceptions and thought in dealing with such topics.[6]

Atatürk certainly seems to have induced strong feelings in some reviewers. Therefore we appreciate the candid remarks of a psychoanalyst of Greek origin whose mother was born and reared in Anatolia but moved to Athens with her family after the Turkish War of Independence, a war that brought catastrophe to Greeks living in Anatolia. This reviewer noted that Atatürk was obviously not his national hero but that, after some soul-searching and self-analysis, he read our book with an ease that surprised him. On the other hand, one reviewer who was an analyst-turned-historian (!) suggested that Atatürk had taken part in the Armenian problem, and compared him indirectly to Hitler. This was purely transference to Atatürk.

Our book pointed out the differences between reparative and destructive leaders who are charismatic and narcissistic.[7] We claim that Atatürk was a prime example of the former since, having been born into a house of mourning, he fantasied about saving his grieving mother, and this fantasy gave him the impetus to save his motherland. There is evidence for his wanting to repair and idealize his followers without devaluing or killing another group in order to feel superior. Hitler operated in the opposite way, using aggression in order to bolster his and his followers' self-esteem, and was thus an extreme example of the destructive leader. The invocation of Hitler's name in discussing Atatürk indicates the reviewer's need to project some hidden inner dread onto an imagined Atatürk quite different from the real one we studied and wrote about.

Some critics, who were not themselves psychoanalysts, claimed that our approach was reductionist, accounting for everything by reference to unconscious instinctual forces. The work of Erik Erikson and other rigorous historical scholarship should suffice to counter this accusation, but some analysts, notably J. E. Mack, continue to warn against reductionism, considering it a most pernicious pitfall in the writing of psychoanalytic biography.[8] A. Falk argues that reductionism should not be equated with the "nothing but" fallacy and adds that it is in fact "a legitimate scientific method because, in truth, all science is reductionist."[9]

Our approach to *The Immortal Atatürk* required examination of his entire life with the assessment of the strength of his instinctual drives, the location of any developmental arrests, reconstruction of his infantile rescue fantasies, and consideration of infantile conflicts and the child's way of dealing with them, ways of adapting, and the nature of the identity crisis at adolescence. Our study also probed the nature of internal responses to external trauma and the handling of midlife issues, as well as psychic transformations and the reaction to aging and the approach of death. We looked at our subject's psychodynamics developmentally. Recent advances in theories of object relations, demonstrating how a cohesive sense of self is established, have enriched our approach to psychoanalytic biography.

Although some of our critics who were not analysts declared our approach Freudian, we are obviously fully aware of the enormous expansion of the field of psychoanalysis since Freud concluded his pioneering work, and of the need to incorporate wider psychoanalytic understanding. Psychoanalysis and Freud are no longer synonymous. Further misunderstandings occur when a nonanalyst relies on theoretical papers without reference to clinical material. The psychoanalyst Ives Hendrick has written: "Psychoanalysis is misused by intellectuals, who argue its validity as if it were a philosophy, an ethical system, a set of theories; such discussions . . . seem alien and unproductive to the analyst himself, whose primary convictions originate in what his patients have told him."[10]

We would be the last to deny that there are any problems in psychoanalytic biography. To understand these difficulties, compare the task of an analyst's writing the biography of one of his or her analysands with that of writing the life story of a long-dead leader who was never psychoanalyzed. In psychoanalysis, a patient's history unfolds before the analyst during many sessions, and by the end of the treatment, the analyst feels that he or she has the patient's total biography, including previously unconscious motivations, fantasies, and defenses—and adaptations to them. Formerly repressed material has become available and new material has been constructed. An analyst writing his or her analysand's biography would add meaning to the life story from the subject's "internal reality." Two examples of such inquiries are *What Do You Get When You Cross a Dandelion with a Rose?* and *Six Steps in the Treatment of Borderline Personality Organization*, although it must be admitted that a literally total biography is not attainable.[11]

Freud suggested using the archeologist's model, the restoration by the analyst of pieces of the puzzle that are missing.[12] The analyst may be justified in filling in the missing pieces of the patient's experience and may approach the truth very closely if what he or she supplies fits well into the tapestry of material apparent in the patient's life. An analyst writing his or her successfully analyzed patient's psychobiography can offer data not available to any other writer. The assumption is that the total history of the subject, in the sense used here, can be obtained only through clinical psychoanalysis and by no other means such as simple interviews or perusal of the record of factual milestones of the life in question.

The method of clinical psychoanalysis, whether in treating or in gathering biographical data about the patient, follows certain principles and brings the analyst and analysand together in a highly specific way. Using Harry Sullivan's terminology, David Rapaport referred to this as "the participant-observation variant of the method of inter-personal relation," adding that this particular type of interpersonal relationship is nonindirective, using free association; is interpretive-genetic; and analyzes defenses.[13] In analysis much information is communicated nonverbally; the trained analyst is sensitive to the revelations of gesture, intonation, and syntax. The analyst also is on the alert for the repetition of patterns the patient developed in childhood in relation to those who were then important to him or her, notably family members. These patterns reappear in daily living, and in dreams and transference neuroses. Free association and the message of repeated patterns will not, however, yield a total history unless the repeated patterns are connected also with the transference, in which the patient displaces them onto the analyst. Rapaport noted that when techniques "are tied up to the concept of transference they are specifically psychoanalytic."[14]

The question remains as to how the biography of a leader who was never analyzed can be called psychoanalytic. Diaries and letters, added to what is known of the subject's political philosophy, artistic productions, and acts, tell much about a public figure, and the story of the subject's youth and growing achievements is often common knowledge. In the case of subjects not long dead, it may be possible to interview persons who had been close to them, or had been affected by them. (This was a very useful source in preparing our book on Atatürk.) Besides citing factual data, a psychoanalytic biography tries to grasp and interpret the unconscious meaning of what does come to light. Since so much depends on the skill of the biographer-analyst, there is always the possibility of a "wild analysis."

It is hard to gain information that will lead to "the royal road of the unconscious."[15] Even if the subject's dreams are known, his or her associations to them are not. The task is obviously easier when symbolic expression of the subject's inner world has been left in artistic productions. The most difficult aspect of a psychoanalytic biography concerns the area of transference neurosis and the reconstruction of unconscious fantasies.

If we limit the scope of psychoanalysis to cases in which we have the benefit of a transference neurosis, we cannot apply the theory to the biography of someone never treated on the analyst's couch. We may ask, however, if we can find substitutes for the transference neurosis and be reasonably sure of the meaning of repeated patterns without it. Many psychoanalysts are optimistic about the availability of substitutes for the transference neurosis and those free associations that let us understand unconscious material.[16] Niederland found Heinrich Schliemann's "language exercises," in which Schliemann discovered unconscious wishes and dreams in sentences written to master a new language, very like free associations.[17] After all,

transferences occur in everyday life, and given everyday transferences in which patterns clearly relate to known childhood
events, we can be reasonably sure about the nature of these
patterns without the close-up participant-observer evaluation
possible in a transference neurosis.

For example, we are struck by Atatürk's fascination with the
sun. The cover of our book shows him silhouetted against it,
and the book's original title was "The Savior Sun." His public
utterances were full of references to the sun and its warmth and
brightness, and this was a signal for the psychoanalyst. However, we missed a clue; only after the book's publication did we
recognize, tardily, the meaning of the name Şemsi, which is
"the illuminator," being derived from the Arabic word for sun,
and which also was the name of a man critically important to
Atatürk in his youth.

The devout mother of the young Mustafa had insisted that
he attend religious school, but his father, shortly before he died,
made it possible for his son to attend secular school under a
teacher named Şemsi Efendi, who seems to have become for the
seven-year-old boy a badly needed substitute for a father lost
during the oedipal period and idealized in spite of his lack of
success and addiction to alcohol. The cogency of the name was
brought out in a review of our book by Kemal Karpat in the
American Historical Review; although opposed to psychoanalytic formulations, Karpat, a Turk, noted that "Atatürk referred to the sun and its life-giving power in many of his
speeches."[18]

Analysts may be optimistic for another reason about biography that can be considered psychoanalytic. Little has been
written about the usefulness in this connection of countertrans-

ference, which complements transference, although Mack, Falk, and Loewenberg provide exceptions.[19] Lacking the benefit of the transference neurosis with a subject who has not been analyzed (and a personal inclusion within that transference), the biographer is likely to seek a substitute in countertransference thoughts and feelings about the subject.

We assume that to call a biography psychoanalytic we must know how the writer deals with this countertransference. A psychoanalyst (or someone who has been well psychoanalyzed) will be uniquely able to handle this; failure to note and analyze countertransference may be an obstacle. At the outset of our project on Atatürk, we probed our motivation for undertaking it and gave careful attention to what he meant to us. Moreover, we believe that writing in collaboration may help deal with countertransference issues. The involvement of other writers, especially those from other disciplines, can provide checks and balances.

A biographer at work lives with the mental image of his or her subject, and the mental representation of Atatürk was a valued companion to us during the seven years of work on his life story. When our book was published, the dean of the University of Virginia School of Medicine gave a reception for us. A night to remember with great pleasure, it marked the end of our association with Atatürk, and that night one of us dreamt of newspapers written in many different languages, all announcing Atatürk's death. Although he felt sad in his dream, when he remembered it the next day he knew that he could now let his distinguished countryman rest in peace and could pass, like his coauthor, to other work.

6 History versus Biography

Shabtai Teveth

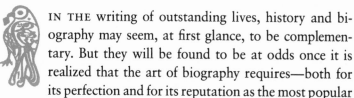IN THE writing of outstanding lives, history and biography may seem, at first glance, to be complementary. But they will be found to be at odds once it is realized that the art of biography requires—both for its perfection and for its reputation as the most popular of nonfiction literary forms—careful selection and an appealing, yet sensible, blend of evidence and poetic license. In fact, these demands create in the biographer's mind a sharp conflict between biography's two principal elements: the writing of a life and the writing of history. Indeed, one may rightly refer to this clash as a case of history versus biography.

History deals with events. But events, we all know, mean different things to different people. The event that can drastically change one life can just as well leave no mark whatsoever on another. War is a good example: some who take part in it are marked by the experience for life, whereas for others it proves but a passing episode. That one event does not necessarily play the same role in two different lives will be found to be true even in regard to great statesmen whose lives are closely interwoven with the events of their times. Which of these events should be given precedence: those that changed the hero's life or the ones that altered the course of history? Even the biographer of a minor historical figure is familiar with this dilemma.

Nowhere is this dilemma more challenging than in David

Ben-Gurion's case.[1] Any serious biographer is bound to recognize early on that his life almost totally coincided, at least from 1921 on, with the history of Zionism and of the Israeli state. In other words Ben-Gurion's life cannot properly be told without telling the history of Zionism, and vice versa. Yet such an enterprise, filling as it would many thick volumes, could hardly be considered biography in the orthodox sense. Are we to include in Ben-Gurion's life all of Zionism's main events, or only those that left their mark on him? History demands the first, although the requirements of selection and appealing narrative suggest the latter.

Lytton Strachey, I would imagine, can rightly be referred to as the apostle of selection. To satisfy lucidity, poetic figment, and brevity—his gods—he selected only those episodes in the lives of his Eminent Victorians that best highlighted their singular characteristics. But what was fine and admirable for miniature portraits of Florence Nightingale and Cardinal Manning, or even Elizabeth and Essex, would hardly do for a Churchill or a Lenin. Even Solzhenitsyn's *Lenin in Zurich,* penetrating as it may be, is only a sketch. In all these, history gets short shrift—too short. History wants neither sketches nor miniatures but rather insists on full-length portraits, in which monograms done in lace are clearly legible.

But the rivalry between the muse of history and the muse of biography does not end here. They both appreciate personal details, and neither will give up on mentioning Caesar's prowess as a lover and a swimmer, or Beethoven's growing loss of hearing. Both muses recognize a connection between their hero's achievements or failures and his life story. Yet they are not of one mind as to the importance or the scope of this connec-

tion. History, undoubtedly, would have given Caesar and Beethoven their proper place even if the first had been a cripple and
the latter had ears as sharp as a rabbit's. The Ninth Symphony,
history would argue, stands by itself, and that is the main thing.
Biography, however, would be twice as enthusiastic about the
symphony because it was conceived in total deafness and would
inquire to what extent the orchestration and particularly the
soprano's role are indebted to this deafness. Furthermore, this
muse would research relentlessly the nature of Beethoven's
deafness, and whether its origin was hereditary syphilis. The
biographer, more than the historian, would strive to understand the relations between Caesar and his friends and adversaries as the motive, and perhaps the compass, of the endeavor.

Thus, the disagreement on events does not abate when personal details are at issue. History concerns itself with the fact
that Ben-Gurion drew conclusions from *Mein Kampf*, whereas
to the biographer the story that in August 1933, at a short stop
in Munich's railway terminal, Ben-Gurion bought only Hitler's
book and Sprinzak cigarettes is of value, this story showing
how much sharper than his colleagues was Ben-Gurion's political sense. The same would apply to the detailed accounts of
the groceries with which Ben-Gurion fed himself in November
1938 in London: "ham, canned beef, tomatoes, lettuce, eggs
and cheese." Trivial, yet how well this information helps the
biographer in describing the loneliness of Ben-Gurion, who ate
in his hotel room and there listened to the radio speeches by
Hitler and Chamberlain, speeches that decided the fate of the
world and the fate of both Europe's Jews and Zionism. The
biographer must therefore decide which personal details are
truly important: only those that left their impact on history or

also those that define and characterize the hero and add color to the narrative.

There is no ready-made compromise. It is up to the biographer to reconcile these conflicting demands, to impose on them a personal solution, knowing full well that no matter what is done in this regard he or she will be accused of committing a crime. Should selection and narrative be favored, the biographer will feel the wrath of historians; should history be given pride of place, readers will be scared away.

In a way it is the biographer's object all sublime, to paraphrase Gilbert, to let the punishment fit the crime. One's ability to let both history and biography represent themselves will decide the degree of one's art. Generally speaking, the less offensive he or she is to either history or biography, the better. Yet, sound advice as this undoubtedly is—is it practical? No. And that is why, to this writer's mind, the biographer who can fully acquit himself or herself in "doing" the life of any major historical figure, let alone one suspected of genius, has yet to be born.

There is a third approach open to the biographer, a very tempting one: to regard "life" as drama. But far from making the biographer's task easier, this option renders it, if this is at all imaginable, far more difficult. For as if two conflicting elements were not enough, this course introduces yet a third. In drama, the argument goes, the hero must be on stage in full view of the audience, if not always then at least most of the time. (Brecht, who once argued to the contrary, clamoring for a play with no hero, was unwilling or unable, great dramatist that he was, to produce one himself.) Now, if biography is to be taken for a play, then the hero must be in evidence on nearly every page. This dictum of the hero's ubiquity leaves little room for historical background (that is, the empty stage, or several pages without the hero), thus further aggravating the biographer's crimes against history. And this is only for starters. For drama, with its strong taste for struggle, would further narrow the field of dramatis personae and events included in the biography to those with which the hero comes to grips directly.

To do justice to the broader backdrop, the biographer as a dramatist will have to resort to "on-the-job" training. In other words, he or she will have to incorporate historical information into the dramatic plot. Robert Graves has shown, in *I, Claudius,* and still better in *Wife to Mr. Milton,* how this can be done. The hero either "exploits" the major figures and events that bear on his life or "is exploited" by them. In the case of a bold and imaginative national leader, this technique would involve the events he or she created, used, played with, or even rode the crest of. The catch here is obviously a simple one: if this dramatic rule is to be kept, few candidates will be found fit to star in a biography of this sort, one in which history and plot are at peace with each other.

In this sense the biographer of Ben-Gurion is rather fortunate: Ben-Gurion excelled in what he himself called "exploiting disaster," that is, turning adversity into advantage. Thus Ben-Gurion provides his biographer with plenty of events from which to choose without the latter running the risk of giving too much offense to history.

To understand Ben-Gurion's political thinking, one must keep in mind that he was born into what was called, by him and by many other Zionists, "the Jewish disaster"—the pogroms and general misery that were, for many centuries, the lot of Jewry, especially in the central and eastern parts of Europe. His singularity was encapsulated in his view of this disaster as a fount of strength, and in his single-mindedness in harnessing it—the way one would wish to turn nothingness into substance, darkness into light, disadvantage into advantage—to the chariot of Zionism. Furthermore, Ben-Gurion set out to fulfill this unique mission with the greatest possible urgency. His fear of "the destruction of Jewry," in Europe by Hitler and in Palestine by Arabs, proved to be, throughout the 1930s, the compass and the engine behind his political thinking. "Disaster," Zionism's strength, was the "lever," as he put it, by which he expected the Zionist dream to be fulfilled. In March 1936, he laid down that Zionism must immediately "begin the policy of a Jewish state." However, the Jewish state was not the end but the means, yet another "lever" to enable "in a minimum of time a maximum of Jewish immigrants" to come to Palestine, and there to create a Jewish majority.

The Arab Revolt, which broke out in April 1936 and lasted three years, threatened the very existence of the Yishuv—the Jewish community of Palestine—then 400,000 strong. Unlike many who feared the Yishuv's collapse, Ben-Gurion greeted the danger heartily, as if it were a heaven-sent challenge to his special talent for turning adversity into advantage. In a spate of imagination and energy, and against vehement opposition within his own party and the Yishuv as a whole, he set about using the revolt to launch his "Jewish state policy." The Arab economic boycott would enable the Yishuv, hitherto dependent on Arab farm produce and Arab workers, to develop into a self-sustaining community, what he termed a "Jewish economy." The constant Arab raids on Jewish settlements would facilitate the strengthening of the Yishuv's defense infrastructure as the groundwork for the army of the future state. And the closure of Palestine's two Arab-manned ports, at Jaffa and Haifa, would pave the way for the improvisation of an off-shore port in Tel Aviv, then the country's only Jewish town. This "Jewish port," both as a symbol and a physical asset, was to him the most important step toward independence. On May 17, 1936, only a day after the port opened for business, Ben-Gurion noted in his diary: "Had there been no loss of life—for which there is no recompense—all the economic destruction would have justified giving the [Arab] rioters a prize for their share in this wonderful creation."

Having proven his mettle as a "disaster-exploiter" par excellence, Ben-Gurion was ready to apply his concept of "disaster means strength" to the European theater. He presaged the Nazi "destruction" of Europe's Jews as early as January 1934 and repeatedly warned that time was running out for them. As Hitler gathered power, Ben-Gurion called on Zionist parties and world Zionist organizations alike to turn "disaster . . . to productive force" and "misery," another "political resource," into a "lever." The destruction of European Jewry, he told his party, was an accelerating factor "in the implementation of our enterprise." In May 1936, he explained to his political colleagues: "We want Hitler destroyed, but while he lasts—it is in our interest to exploit this fact for the build-up of Palestine."

The Yishuv in Palestine, he argued, was the only haven for Europe's Jews, their one and only rescue. Not wishing to wait for history to prove him right, Ben-Gurion energetically explored a number of avenues of rescue while there still was time. In 1934 he negotiated with Palestinian Arab leaders the creation of a federation with Syria, Iraq, and Transjordan, on the understanding that the Jewish state would be entitled to bring in six, even eight, million Jews; in 1937 he was willing to accept partition and a tiny Jewish state, only because it would at least be free to open its gates to Hitler's would-be victims. His idea of "exploiting" Hitler was that Jewish and world opinion recognize the rightness of his cause, the Jewish state, and help to set it up as quickly as possible. But all his predictions and warnings fell on deaf ears.

It was his custom to state, or indeed overstate, his position in stark alternatives; as the years passed and doomsday drew near for Europe's Jews, Ben-Gurion used ever bolder language. His total dedication to the "historic interest," sometimes even to the exclusion of the individual, found extreme expression in December 1938 when, in a reductio ad absurdum, he told his party's Central Committee: "Were I to know that the rescue of all German Jewish children could be achieved by their transfer to England, and of only half their number by transfer to Palestine, I would opt for the latter—because our concern is not only the personal interest of these children, but the historic interest of the Jewish people."

This brutal formulation reflected his bitterness at the world's indifference to Jewish misery, revealed by the Evian Conference; at Britain's betrayal of Zionism, following the horrors of *Kristallnacht*; and at the blatant hypocrisy of the British government in claiming that the Jewish question could be solved in Angola, in Guyana, or elsewhere, all the while refusing to allow the rescue of 10,000 German Jewish children by sending them to Palestine. The horrors of the Holocaust were still in the future, unimaginable by Ben-Gurion or by anyone else. He knew very well that his formulation was purely theoretical and that there was no hope of rescuing the German Jewish children anyway. In using words to which later events gave a different and unintended meaning, his purpose was to hammer home the axiom that a true rescue of the Jewish people was possible only in Palestine, and that the only real choice that confronted European Jewry, children and adults alike, was for half and even less to be saved in Palestine, or not to be saved at all.

It was this belief that drove him to militate throughout the war years for a Jewish state, and to inspire and orchestrate Hitler's survivors—whom he was the first Zionist leader to meet, in 1944 and 1945—in voicing the single demand for a Jewish state. If the establishment of Israel in May 1948 can be seen, at least in part, as directly resulting from the Holocaust, then Ben-Gurion could have claimed this to be his most stupendous "exploitation." Surely no one would dispute that the Holocaust followed by a Jewish state was better than the Holocaust without Israel. Yet to steer such a course when the Holocaust was in progress, to embed his policy in the minds of the broken refugees from the death camps, to motivate them to proclaim the Zionist cause because humanity owed it to them—this took a great deal more than mere courage and imperviousness. It called for a very special sort of person, one whose vision was soaring unarrested and whose self-control was absolute. That Ben-Gurion was such a man, that only twice was he unable to stop his tears on meeting the survivors, that there was a great roaring inside him and—well, that is what his biography should be all about.

7   The Biographical Element in Political History

Uriel Dann

I AM a student of political history and not a biographer. But I have a penchant for the role of the individual. It is purely a matter of preference; there is no principle involved, and of course I try not to lose sight of the nameless forces that go far to shape the human destiny. All the same, each major theme that has so far taken my attention has one person who occupies center stage: General Qasim as the "Sole Leader" during the first years of the Iraqi republic, Amir 'Abdallah in Transjordan under the mandate, and King Husayn in Jordan during its struggle for survival. This inclination must be my personal preference, and not something peculiar to the Middle Eastern political scene, for a study on Western Europe in the eighteenth century that recently kept me busy for three years also centers on an individual, a Baron von Münchhausen. (He is not the famous teller of tall stories, I hasten to add, but a distant relation.)

I do not consciously couple my work as a political historian with any discipline other than history—be it political science, or economics, or sociology, or anthropology, or psychology. This may be the result of my lack of formal training in these disciplines; or else, my lack of training may be the result of my never having felt the urge to take them up. However that may be, if this makes me a "pragmatic" historian, that tag is as good as any. (A reviewer once called me a "pragmatic historian" in this context, in no unfriendly spirit.) And if you think the deficiency diminishes the value of my work, then I just have to face my critics, inductively, point by point to be sure. Face the argument as a whole, conceptually, I cannot; I do not feel competent to plead whether or not a political historian must also be trained as a political scientist, or in any other of the additional disciplines I mentioned above.

As to the distinction between biography and political history with a biographical bias, the key is obviously relevant to the overall theme of the work, but some pondering is still useful. Respecting certain societies during certain periods, such as Western Europe in the nineteenth century, the ordinary measure of common sense is a fair guide for the historian. Take for instance Benjamin Disraeli. An outstanding trait of his personality was his need for women. Not, indeed, sexually; he was no womanizer. But he constantly needed female sympathy, admiration, even mothering. Yet Disraeli the politician and statesman was not appreciably bent by this trait. You will not find his sister and his wife, or Henrietta Sykes and Lady Bradford, given any prominence in a political history of Victorian England, not even one focusing on the leaders of that time. Try, however, to remove women from Robert Blake's wonderful biography of Disraeli and see the havoc—and Lord Blake is as fine a political historian as any today.

The Middle East in the twentieth century poses a more difficult problem; at least, most political societies there do so most of the time. The reason is clear. The phenomenon of the "hero"—not necessarily a term of approval—is much more general in the Middle East than in the West, for reasons that are a major object of independent research. (The giants of the West during the first half of this century are not characteristic of their society over a longer span.) In our present context, this phenomenon, the prevalence of a hero, makes the task of the political historian more complicated or, if you like, more idiosyncratic. Amir ʿAbdallah loved chess. He also had a trick of assuming a diffident smile when talking to important Britishers. King Husayn goes in (or perhaps used to go in) for speed driving. He divorced his first wife with considerable cruelty, such as is not usually associated with him. General Qasim loved to tour the streets of Baghdad at night, Harun al-Rashid–like. All this is meat for the biographer. Does it have a rightful place in political histories? Considering the societies in which these persons moved, I think it has. But what place? And, more important, how can I ensure that I pursue what is after all a penchant of mine in a manner conforming to the agreed rules of our profession? And, with respect, what are these rules?

At the risk of appearing trite, I will make a few points. The first is, I believe, the most controversial, and for that reason I bring it first, and not because it is more important than others. Whether you are a biographer or a political historian with a biographer's bias, you should have a liking for your chief actor. Of course you must preserve your critical faculty—the more so, since you have, by my definition, that liking. But unless you develop a certain affinity, a human fellow-feeling, I think you cannot have the necessary empathy. This underlying liking is in most cases a sort of dowry that the historians bring to their task. After all, they rarely choose a theme with which they have not been well acquainted for some time. There are exceptions: I myself was entirely ignorant of Gerlach von Münchhausen's existence when I began work on the relations between Hanover and England under George II, and lo and behold, the study turned out to have as much a biographical bias as anything I had ever touched on twentieth-century Iraq, Transjordan, or Jordan. I quickly grew a liking, mixed with respect, for the man—the leading minister of Hanover to be sure, but neither a great statesman nor a paragon in any other way. And he had as much charisma as a dish cloth. Conversely, I know that I could not do anything of value that centered on Saddam Husayn's Iraq, or Nasser's Egypt or, for that matter, on Prussia under Frederick the Great. I dislike the protagonists, and that is that. My own limitations need not apply to everybody. But I do not recall any biography that I valued when I sensed that the biographer was fundamentally antagonistic to the hero. Here you may ask, what about biographies of Hitler, or Mussolini, or Stalin—those which, by professional consensus, are of high standing? I have no ready answer. With some hesitation I suggest that these works are exceptional in that the biographers strove to give a rational fundament to their previous loathing.

Empathy should follow, provided you put in a lot of time and work over a long period. Empathy may become an obsession that reaches a climax as the job in hand nears fulfillment. The obsession soon fades; I have never heard of a historian suffering permanent damage. But I shall never forget, nor did my wife, how I once awoke in the small hours of the night believing that I was ʿAbd al-Karim Qasim. The delusion passed.

Affinity and empathy are worthless professionally, as opposed to, perhaps, aesthetically, unless they are founded on knowledge—the knowledge of evidence or "facts." I dislike belaboring the obvious, but there are points that I still have to stress: First, the effort involved in the search. This sounds elementary; it should be, but it is not. Second, the distinction between what your mind must register while you prepare your study and what finally passes all sieves to enter your product. Regarding the former, truly all that comes to your mill except the palpably trivial is grist. (There is no ironclad definition of what is palpably trivial, but we are expected, after all, to exercise some judgment.) I think that it is the blurring of this distinction that gives "facts" the slightly derogatory tang that they commonly have in the profession. There is a phrase in a recent essay on psychohistory that expresses disdain for the "mere recital of facts."[1] Apart from the context (which I do not find convincing), the idea itself that a "mere recital of facts" is something to be held in disdain disturbs me. Of course we do not want a chronicle of disconnected facts, but is this at issue? We certainly cannot do without considering the secret self, the inner myth, particularly not in biography. Being children of our times, we are less likely to ignore the secret self than to overrate it. Yet I believe that one ounce of fact is worth a ton of speculation. I also believe that "le bon dieu est dans le petit détail"—I have just found the sentiment in Professor Shlomo Ben-Ami's foreword to the first issue of the *Mediterranean Historical Review*. Incidentally, the Germans say, "der Teufel steckt im Detail." God or the devil—it depends on whether you get your detail right or wrong.

You must absorb the ambience through proficiency in the language and personal acquaintance with the surroundings associated with your theme. The former, linguistic proficiency, should be a matter of course, but it is not, and again I will leave it at that. Regarding the latter, the recent years have been both kind and unkind to Israelis. The opening of Egypt is priceless; Morocco may follow soon, and possibly it has already opened up to some extent. Iran has been closed to us since 1979. Turkey is less accessible to Israelis than it used to be. Saddest of all is the increasing difficulty for us Jewish Israelis in creating, and maintaining, meaningful contact with the Arab sector, not merely in the West Bank and Gaza, but even this side of the Green Line. This last phenomenon has of course a significance that transcends our professional interest.

What of the potential sources? The national archives of Middle Eastern countries are closed, so far as I know, to most scholars studying the period since World War I. Still, there is a trend toward greater liberality. Israel adheres to the thirty-years rule, by and large. Jordanian files in eastern Jerusalem and elsewhere in the West Bank are mostly open to research. Professor Hanna Batatu has had access to Iraqi police and security files. Egyptian authorities may give access as a favor to the royal archives at ʿAbdin Palace. Jordanian archives seem to have become more accessible, in certain fields. I will add that for the *political* historian of the modern Middle East the Western public archives are a pretty good substitute, with their thirty-years rule, and with the even more recent official material that is continuously declassified in the United States along quite liberal lines.

I deem it especially important to put in a word for the much-maligned Arabic press. If there is one professional achievement of which I am proud, it is the use to which I have put the Iraqi press of Qasim's time, and if there is one negative criticism of my work that I think downright ignorant, it is the criticism that I made use of that press. Indeed, journalism in the Arab world is often the object of censorship, regimentation, bribery, harassment, and outright persecution. But publishers, editors, and plain correspondents have as a matter of self-preservation grown an intelligence superior to that of the authorities, and they often find a way to deliver their messages—whether of fact or of opinion. At least, I would advise the historian to assume that they have found the way, and to look for it. The quest may be astoundingly rewarding. (Lebanon is a special case, in regard to its press as in so much else. Here the researcher's overriding need is to determine who directs whom, and to what extent.)

Interviews with actors on the stage are an important source in Arab countries that is largely denied to the Israeli historian—largely, though by no means entirely so. I would have given a lot to have talked to General Qasim or to King Husayn. I would have to evaluate their knowledgeability, their frankness, and their truthfulness, but the ability to do so is a test that every historian must pass. For me, it is not to be. I find some comfort in that I am spared one temptation that faces the historian who makes a point of cultivating living sources. I know one colleague, and an eminent colleague at that, whom I suspect of dealing with undue leniency with high-placed interviewees who might, if offended, withhold further cooperation. But mine may be merely a case of sour grapes.

Lastly, I love to gaze at portraits. A good many of course do not tell a thing, but I find that the majority do. And here I will mention the caveats. First, the message of a portrait is personal; your man, or woman, looks at you benevolently, or cunningly, or stupidly—it is all the same photograph, and the reading depends on your individuality, and often on your predisposition. Second, and this of course is an external factor, the message of a portrait depends on the circumstances in which it was taken. Look at Qasim in 1958 and in 1962. The ravages of four years of power, and the corruption of that power, stare from his eyes into ours. But then, the earlier portrait was taken in repose, whereas the latter shows a demagogue in full action. Who can say for certain how far the two are comparable?[2] And who can say whether the frightened little boy propped up against his frightening father's side has something to tell us about Mohammad Reza Shah Pahlavi fifty years after?[3] Still, trying to read portraits is a fascinating game, and I would not do without it.

This brings me to autobiographies, or memoirs, and their usefulness to the political historian of the modern Middle East, as distinct from the biographer. As to the incidence—not too bad, so far as my personal interest as a historian is concerned: ʿAbdallah's *Mudhakkirat* and the *Takmila*, King Husayn's *Uneasy Lies the Head* and *Ma Guerre avec Israël*, and works by a few Transjordanian-Jordanian and a host of Iraqi politicians. The direct gain to the political historian is remarkably small. But as you read between the lines, you do gain in the understanding of political processes at work, beyond the actor-writer's personality. ʿAbdallah describing the stewardship of the chief British representative at Amman after 1924, Lieutenant Colonel Henry Cox, as "a difficult time for . . . the Hashemite family," when "much patience was necessary," provides a shattering understatement that helps to explain why ʿAbdallah proved indestructible. And King Husayn abstaining from mentioning with even a single word the Suez Canal nationalization in July 1956 shows how ill-conceived his Arab-nationalist (*qawmi*) period seemed to him after a few years and, by implication, how ill it must have sat on him even in 1956.

I have said what I wanted to say. I think it is relevant, or else I would not have said it. But I do not want you to think that I have lost my sense of proportion. Gibbon says somewhere that the cardinal virtues in a historian are diligence and accuracy. (I have failed in my attempt to locate the quotation; hence I certainly lack diligence, and probably accuracy.) Gibbon was a political historian with a penchant for the role of the individual, like myself. He was not a historian of the Middle East, but this gives me no special latitude.

8   A Sampler of Biography and Self-Narrative

Martin Kramer

IN A comprehensive survey of Middle Eastern historiography written some fifteen years ago, the historian Albert Hourani determined that "there are almost no satisfactory biographies, even in the modern period." That verdict is less apt today, for there are now numerous biographies, influenced by most major schools of biographical writing, that do satisfy more demanding tastes. Still, major gaps remain. The aim of this sampler is to direct the reader to a number of books in English that are representative of various approaches to biography and self-narrative. This selection is offered as an abbreviated guide to anyone who wishes to compare these approaches, and a practical reading list for courses on Middle Eastern biography, self-narrative, personalities, and leadership. The suggestions are for readers with a primary interest in the modern period. Preference is given to American over British editions, and to the most recent editions or reprints.

The best biographies of Middle Eastern subjects are those of political intellectuals—persons who shaped the ideas of nationalism, reformism, and revolution. The mark left by these figures was often more profound than that of the leaders and rulers who were their contemporaries. And unlike the leaders and rulers, many political intellectuals have left private papers that thoroughly document the evolution of their ideas and politics.

The most prominent figure of this kind was Sayyid Jamal al-Din "al-Afghani," reckoned as the intellectual precursor of many of the major trends in modern political thought—from reformism to fundamentalism, from nationalism to Pan-Islam. The amount of writing on Afghani is formidable, with even a published bibliography devoted to studies of him. This biographical endeavor culminated in Nikki R. Keddie's *Sayyid Jamal ad-Din "al-Afghani": A Political Biography* (Berkeley and Los Angeles: University of California Press, 1972). Keddie's definitive book, which rests on detective work in many European and Middle Eastern archives, succeeded in dispelling the last wisps of fog that had obscured Afghani's life and works. It is instructive to compare the full biography to Keddie's article, "Sayyid Jamal ad-Din 'al-Afghani': A Case of Posthumous Charisma?," in *Philosophers and Kings: Studies in Leadership*, ed. Dankwart A. Rustow (New York: Braziller, 1970), 148–79. In the article Keddie attempts "a psycho-historical analysis" of Afghani, drawing on theoretical literature on paranoia and its relationship to latent homosexuality. The speculative points made in the article were excluded from the full biography, perhaps because, as Keddie noted, "psychological analyses of heroes are often resented, and doubly so when a non-Muslim Westerner writes about a Muslim Easterner."

A second example, of comparable worth, is Hamid Algar's *Mirza Malkum Khan: A Study in the History of Iranian Modernism* (Berkeley and Los Angeles: University of California Press, 1973), which painstakingly reconstructs the winding life of a leading Iranian Muslim reformer and reveals it to be something quite different than historians had hitherto assumed. The author's tone is clearly hostile toward his subject, who is cast in the role of manipulative charlatan, but the charlatanry is documented with impressive thoroughness.

Yet another example is William Cleveland's *Islam against the West: Shakib Arslan and the Campaign for Islamic Nationalism* (Austin: University of Texas Press, 1985), a biography of still another Muslim intellectual and activist, who spent the decades between World War I and II in Geneva as a pamphleteer for Arab and Muslim independence. This study tends to extend the benefit of the doubt to the subject, who was enmeshed in intrigue and compromising alliances. The language of the book, however, is a model of balance, and the archival research is thorough. Cleveland, it should be noted, is perhaps the only historian of the modern Middle East to regard himself as a biographer. He is the author of an earlier study of another political intellectual, *The Making of an Arab Nationalist: Ottomanism and Arabism in the Life and Thought of Sati' al-Husri* (Princeton: Princeton University Press, 1971); Cleveland is now preparing a biography of George Antonius.

There are a number of other stimulating biographies of intellectuals. Particularly noteworthy is the study by Charles D. Smith, *Islam and the Search for Social Order in Modern Egypt: A Biography of Muhammad Husayn Haykal* (Albany: State University of New York Press, 1983), which is presented as a "social biography." Two examples of shorter studies, which fall somewhere between biography and intellectual portraiture, are Uriel Heyd's *Foundations of Turkish Nationalism: The Life and Teachings of Ziya Gökalp* (London: Luzac, 1950) and Irene L. Gendzier's *The Practical Visions of Ya'qub Sanu'* (Cambridge:

Harvard University Press, 1966). Many of the most important figures in Middle Eastern intellectual history have not yet had their lives written in English, including such central thinkers as Muhammad ʿAbduh and Rashid Rida. There are, however, shorter sketches of such thinkers, the best known being Albert Hourani's *Arabic Thought in the Liberal Age* (Cambridge: Cambridge University Press, 1983).

Autobiographies by intellectuals are numerous, but the available English translations are few. Particularly valuable, therefore, are Salama Musa's *The Education of Salama Musa* (Leiden: Brill, 1961) and Ahmad Amin's *My Life: The Autobiography of an Egyptian Scholar, Writer and Cultural Leader* (Leiden: Brill, 1978). One such work that has always been one of the most popular books for the teaching of Arabic in America is Taha Husayn's autobiography, published in parts and in various editions as *An Egyptian Childhood, The Stream of Days,* and *A Passage to France.* Recently the book has been reinterpreted in Fedwa Malti-Douglas's *Blindness and Autobiography: Al-Ayyam of Taha Husayn* (Princeton: Princeton University Press, 1988), a work that also has much to say on broader questions of self-narrative.

The modern rulers and leaders of the Middle East have been less well served by biographers. In many cases, the necessary source materials are inaccessible, even for rulers whose dynasties have long since disappeared. None of the major modernizing rulers of the nineteenth century has been the subject of a first-rate biography, although the lives of some have been sketched as part of an overall discussion of their reforms. Noteworthy among such works are the studies by Stanford J. Shaw, *Between Old and New: The Ottoman Empire under Sultan Se-*

lim III, 1789–1807 (Cambridge: Harvard University Press, 1971); by L. Carl Brown, *The Tunisia of Ahmad Bey, 1837–1855* (Princeton: Princeton University Press, 1974); and by Afaf Lutfi Sayyid-Marsot, *Egypt in the Reign of Muhammad Ali* (Cambridge: Cambridge University Press, 1984). In each of these books, a powerful individual stands at center stage, although none of these studies is conceived or executed as a full biography. The limitations in writing about palace lives are perhaps best evoked by Franz Babinger in his monumental *Mehmed the Conqueror and His Time* (Princeton: Princeton University Press, 1978): "It is even more difficult to obtain a reliable portrait of Mehmed the man than of Mehmed the ruler. Any attempt to derive a complete picture of his character and personality from the statements of contemporaries and chance observers is a hazardous undertaking. Nearly everything that was said of him in his lifetime reflected either boundless, slavish admiration and deification or hatred and contempt." In such circumstances, the custom has always been to write not just the life but the times, often with emphasis on the latter.

The last and most visible of the palace lives, those lived in the last decades of the nineteenth century, could prove to be exceptions, but they have not yet received scholarly attention. Perhaps the most compelling among them is the "Red Sultan," Abdülhamid II—the remarkable product of a once-great Ottoman palace system in decline, and a personality marked by calculating shrewdness and scarred by fear. His life has inspired a few biographical studies by amateurs. Alma Wittlin's *Abdul Hamid: The Shadow of God* (London: John Lane the Bodley Head, 1940) presents itself as a "psychological study," based "especially on the unpublished testimony of persons who once formed a part of the Sultan's entourage—members of the imperial family, officials, palace-secretaries, sons of members of the Government and women of the Harem." This work has been described more than once as a biographical novel, although it is not without art. The later book by Joan Haslip, *The Sultan: The Life of Abdul Hamid II* (New York: Holt, Rinehart and Winston, 1973), does not take the story much further. The richness of the Ottoman archives, with the large number of administrative and personal documents that the sultan himself generated, now makes Abdülhamid II a prime candidate for a scholarly biography. Nasir al-Din Shah, the Qajar ruler of Iran during roughly the same period, is an equally worthy subject for a biography, and one is now reportedly in preparation by Abbas Amanat. This potential is ably evoked by Ehsan Yar-Shater in "Observations on Nasir al-Din Shah," in *Qajar Iran*, ed. E. Bosworth and C. Hillenbrand (Edinburgh: Edinburgh University Press, 1983), 3–13. There are still no scholarly biographies of the ambitious Khedives Isma'il and 'Abbas Hilmi of Egypt.

The rulers and leaders who rose to preeminence after the collapse of the Ottoman and Qajar empires have inspired a number of amateur and journalistic biographies. Fewer scholarly biographies have been attempted and the distinction between the two approaches is often quite striking. Although historians prefer documentary materials and sometimes would rather wait until their subject has spoken his or her last, journalists are most at home with the interview and actually prefer to examine living and breathing subjects. The great merit of journalistic biographies is that they often contain rare information and insights. Often they are beautifully written and are free of theorizing jargon. Their principal defect is their tendency to judge their subjects with sometimes unabashed partisanship, and always with haste (for journalists must rush to press). It is often a worthwhile exercise to compare biographies by journalists, written at close range, to accounts of the same lives written by scholars more remote from their subjects. The instances that lend themselves to direct comparison are few but will be noted below.

For the Arab Fertile Crescent, many major figures have not yet found their biographers. Particularly striking is the absence of serious biographies for the Hashemites, including Sharif (later King) Husayn and his son Faysal, who ruled briefly in Damascus and established the (short-lived) Hashemite dynasty in Baghdad. Lord Birdwood's *Nuri as-Said: A Study in Arab Leadership* (London: Cassell, 1959) is an openly sympathetic account of one of Faysal's chief lieutenants, based on long talks with the subject. The author, however, chose to avoid inquiry into "the details of family life," because they were of "little interest" to the subject himself, and "I would rather this record was in accordance with the wishes of the great man concerned than that it should offer sensational attraction"—a remarkable concession for any biographer to make to a subject. Later rulers in Baghdad still have few biographers. Uriel Dann's *Iraq under Qassem: A Political History, 1958–1963* (New York: Praeger, 1969) sets the man in his context but is not intended as a full biography. A line of biographers of Saddam Husayn formed quickly after Iraq's invasion of Kuwait in 1990. The best of these works to date is Efraim Karsh and Inari Rautsi's *Saddam Hussein: A Political Biography* (New York: Free Press, 1991).

Jordan's more enduring branch of the Hashemite line has

been considered in Mary C. Wilson's *King Abdullah, Britain and the Making of Jordan* (Cambridge: Cambridge University Press, 1987). This is a hostile portrait of an ʿAbdallah consumed by an ambition that ultimately consumed Palestine as well. However, the work does not pretend to be a full biography and sketches ʿAbdallah only in such detail as its argument requires. For King Husayn, there is only James Lunt's *Hussein of Jordan: Searching for a Just and Lasting Peace* (New York: Morrow, 1989). Lunt does "not doubt that my admiration for the King will be evident"—so much so that he is compelled to add that the biography was not commissioned, although it was "written with the King's agreement."

Two biographies of Syria's president, Hafiz al-Asad, provide an opportunity to compare the work of journalist and scholar. Patrick Seale's *Asad of Syria: The Struggle for the Middle East* (Berkeley and Los Angeles: University of California Press, 1989) is "not an official biography" but one very much indebted to the personal rapport established between the journalist and his subject. Contrast this with Moshe Ma'oz's *Asad: The Sphinx of Damascus* (New York: Weidenfeld and Nicholson, 1988), written at double the distance by an Israeli academic. Few Lebanese leaders have inspirational qualities that transcend sect, but the life of one has been artfully told in Fouad Ajami's *The Vanished Imam: Musa al Sadr and the Shia of Lebanon* (Ithaca: Cornell University Press, 1986). The author has based his work largely on interviews with those who were close to his subject, and the portrait is admiring but not overbearing.

It is difficult to say the same for the work done on Palestinian leaders. Philip Mattar's *The Mufti of Jerusalem: Muhammad Amin al-Husayni and the Palestine Question* (New York: Columbia University Press, 1988) strikes one possible balance of interpretation but is very thin on important and controversial chapters in the mufti's life. Thomas Kiernan's *Arafat: The Man and the Myth* (New York: Norton, 1976) creates a few myths of its own by getting facts wrong. Alan Hart's *Arafat: A Political Biography* (Bloomington: Indiana University Press, 1989) casts its subject in a heroic light; this work is an "epic story" cataloging the "miracle of his leadership" and has embarrassed even some of Arafat's admirers. For Arafat's Palestinian rivals, little material is available. An example of the rather dubious genre of the intelligence biography, which relies on privileged leaks, is Yossi Melman's *The Master Terrorist: True Story of Abu Nidal* (New York: Adama Books, 1986).

Nowhere have the amateur biographers served their subjects so uncritically as in their accounts of the House of Saud. David Howarth's *The Desert King: A Life of Ibn Saud* (London: Collins, 1964) is the most independent-minded study of the founder of the present kingdom, and still it lionizes the "desert king" and mourns the corruption of his heirs. Those heirs have not been examined by discriminating eyes, but the existing studies do include much useful grist. Such is the case with Gerald de Gaury's *Faisal: King of Arabia* (London: Arthur Barker, 1966), which salutes Saudi Arabia's "good fortune in having Faisal, the boy from Najd, now King, as guide." Vincent Sheean's *Faisal: The King and His Kingdom* (Tavistock, England: Butler, 1975) was written out of personal friendship, and this fact clearly shows. Biography by "friends" is perhaps the inevitable first step on the road to more diverse representations but is arguably more an obstacle than a useful preface to critical work.

King Faruq of Egypt has yet to find his biographer, although he would make a fascinating subject given his popular reputation for extravagance and debauchery—and the more important fact that his reign was pivotal to Egypt's transformation by revolution. A rather uneven first effort is Barrie St. Clair McBride's *Farouk of Egypt* (New York: A. S. Barnes, 1968). In contrast, Nasser has been the subject of many biographies, both by journalists and scholars. There is, for example, Jean Lacouture's *Nasser, A Biography* (New York: Knopf, 1973), a lucid account colored, as he says, with a "critical sympathy" for Nasser. Compare it to P. J. Vatikiotis's *Nasser and His Generation* (New York: St. Martin's Press, 1978), which is longer on criticism and shorter on sympathy. Nasser's successor is virtually skewered in David Hirst and Irene Beeson's *Sadat* (London: Faber and Faber, 1981), a work by two journalists that is sometimes little more than an eloquent diatribe against their subject. "Sadat was by no means the world's most absolute ruler," they write, "but his career illustrated, in a remarkable way, how far the personal can predominate over the political and, when the personal is as peculiar as it was in him, what perversities, in the name of policy, can then ensue." Contrast this with Raphael Israeli's *Man of Defiance: A Political Biography of Anwar Sadat* (Totowa, N.J.: Barnes and Noble Books, 1985), which claims only to evoke Sadat's "thinking, his hesitations, his fears, his images and the reasoning behind his acts," without "delving into value judgments of any sort." Still, this work finds him more hero than buffoon.

Atatürk is the subject of a vast amount of biographical writing in Turkish and of two important biographies in English. Lord Kinross's *Atatürk* (New York: Morrow, 1965) is an impressively researched biography that draws on the recollections of many who knew and worked under Atatürk. Its perspective is naturally admiring. The study by Vamik D. Volkan and Norman Itzkowitz, *The Immortal Atatürk: A Psychobiography* (Chicago: University of Chicago Press, 1984), is no less admiring of Atatürk's achievements but seeks to establish a very different explanation of motive by its reliance on psychoanalytic theory.

For Atatürk's Iranian contemporary, Reza Shah, there is nothing comparable. Donald N. Wilber's *Riza Shah Pahlavi: The Resurrection and Reconstruction of Iran, 1878–1944* (Hicksville, N.Y.: Exposition Press, 1975) is an uninspired narrative. Farhad Diba's *Mohammad Mossadegh: A Political Biography* (London: Croom Helm, 1986) is a straightforward narrative based on Mossadegh's writings and on British and American archives. Mossadegh, a complex man, now warrants still more complex treatment. A different approach has been taken in Marvin Zonis's *Majestic Failure: The Fall of the Shah of Iran* (Chicago: University of Chicago Press, 1991), which addresses Mohammad Reza Shah's conduct during the Iranian revolution from a psychoanalytic vantage point. Although the book is not intended as a full biography, it does develop an innovative line of biographical inquiry. At present, Ayatollah Khomeini is the subject only of journalistic treatments: Amir Taheri's *The Spirit of Allah: Khomeini and the Islamic Revolution* (Bethesda, Md.: Adler and Adler, 1986) and Baqer Moin's *Khomeini: Sign of God* (London: Tauris, 1991). Hamid Algar and Marvin Zonis are reportedly working on more thorough studies. In the meantime, it is useful to compare two sketches of Khomeini's early years, one by Michael M. J.

Fischer, "Imam Khomeini: Four Levels of Understanding," in *Voices of Resurgent Islam,* ed. John L. Esposito (New York: Oxford University Press, 1983), 150–74; and the less-speculative and more reverential interpretation by Hamid Algar, "Imam Khomeini, 1902–1962: The Pre-revolutionary Years," in *Islam, Politics, and Social Movements,* ed. Edmund Burke III and Ira M. Lapidus (Berkeley and Los Angeles: University of California Press, 1988), 263–88.

Such biographical portraiture pretends to less than full biography, although the penetrating portrait can be a miniature work of art in the right hands. Majid Khadduri offers two volumes of (rather uncritical) sketches of Middle Eastern leaders: *Arab Contemporaries: The Role of Personalities in Politics* (Baltimore: Johns Hopkins University Press, 1973) and *Arab Personalities in Politics* (Washington, D.C.: Middle East Institute, 1981). More recently, a collection of sketches of Middle Eastern leaders, relating personality to performance in a single crisis, has been assembled by Barbara Kellerman and Jeffrey Z. Rubin, eds. *Leadership and Negotiation in the Middle East* (New York: Praeger, 1988). Finally, over seventy sketches by almost as many hands have been collected by Bernard Reich, ed. *Political Leaders of the Contemporary Middle East and North Africa: A Biographical Dictionary* (New York: Greenwood Press, 1990). The entries are substantial enough to warrant description as sketches and include short bibliographies, providing a useful starting point for students seeking inspiration for assignments.

Students interested in Middle Eastern rulers and leaders should also give due attention to the self-serving autobiographies and memoirs of these leaders, such as Ismail Kemal Bey's

The Memoirs of Ismail Kemal Bey (London: Constable, 1920); Djemal Pasha's *Memories of a Turkish Statesman, 1913–1919* (New York: Arno Press, 1973); King ʿAbdallah's *Memoirs of King Abdullah of Transjordan* (London: Cape, 1950) and the sequel, *My Memoirs Completed "Al Takmilah"* (New York: Longman, 1978); King Husayn's *Uneasy Lies the Head: The Autobiography of His Majesty King Hussein I of the Hashemite Kingdom of Jordan* (New York: Bernard Geis Associates, 1962); Anwar Sadat's *In Search of Identity: An Autobiography* (New York: Harper and Row, 1978); Mohammad Reza Shah's *Mission for My Country* (New York: McGraw-Hill, 1961) and his *Answer to History* (New York: Stein and Day, 1980); and Abu Iyad's *My Home, My Land,* written with Eric Rouleau (New York: Times Books, 1981). The list could be lengthened considerably.

Beyond the world of thinkers and leaders are the men and women usually excluded from history, people who, despite their obscurity, can personify a social order or revolution from below. This kind of telling is often associated with anthropology but also has been done by journalists and even historians. One example of this approach is Dale F. Eickelman's *Knowledge and Power in Morocco: The Education of a Twentieth-Century Notable* (Princeton: Princeton University Press, 1985), which is an anthropologist's view of the way political and social change is played out in the life of one learned man. Roy Mottahedeh's *The Mantle of the Prophet: Religion and Politics in Iran* (New York: Simon and Schuster, 1985) is a historian's telling of the life of an Iranian cleric, one "Ali Hashemi"—"a real person whose wish to remain anonymous I have scrupulously respected." The account is intermingled with discursive asides on Perso-Islamic history and contemporary Iranian culture. Richard Critchfield's *Shahhat: An Egyptian* (Syracuse: Syracuse University Press, 1978) is a journalist's account of events in a young villager's life, as witnessed by the author or recounted to him, a study that borders on literature. "In the end," writes Critchfield, "all study of human beings lies in a borderland between science and art and the difference between the journalist and the anthropologist is one of degree; one mixes some science with his art, the other some art with his science." This apology has not been universally accepted. The book should be read with the article by Timothy Mitchell, "The Invention and Reinvention of the Egyptian Peasant," *International Journal of Middle Eastern Studies* 22 (May 1990): 129–50, a critique that accuses Critchfield of racism, plagiarism, and ahistoricism (this last charge, of course, being the privilege of the historian). This article will not be the last word in the controversy.

The amount of published self-narrative by the people overlooked by history is small, and even less is available in English translation. These works include Reşat Nuri Güntekin's *The Autobiography of a Turkish Girl*, trans. Wyndham Deedes (London: Allen and Unwin, 1949), and Muhammad ʿAli Jamalzadeh's *Isfahan Is Half the World: Memories of a Persian Boyhood*, trans. W. L. Heston (Princeton: Princeton University Press, 1983). A self-narrative, of course, need not be literary, or even the work of a literate person; it can sometimes be presented through the mediation of a listener. One example is Vincent Crapanzano's *Tuhami: Portrait of a Moroccan* (Chicago: University of Chicago Press, 1980), a highly experimental account of the author's encounter with an illiterate Moroccan

Arab tilemaker. Most of the text is an annotated self-narrative by Tuhami himself, a revelation rich in allusion and embellishment, so that *Tuhami* is as much a self-portrait as a portrait. The serious student of biography will want to range even further for comparisons and inspiration, from biographical writing on subjects in other cultural contexts to the burgeoning theoretical and methodological literature and the specialized journals devoted to biography. Any interested reader will have no difficulty finding a point of entry into this literature. A beginning can be made in the outstanding periodic bibliography of the quarterly journal *Biography,* which is published by the Biographical Research Center. Less-systematic inspiration can be had by browsing in specialty bookstores, like New York's Biography Bookshop.

Supplementary reading may be found in the biographies of the many figures from beyond the Middle East who left their impress on the history of the region. Notable among these figures are the English, from proconsuls to travelers, who made careers of the Middle East. Their diaries and letters, often preserved in their entirety, have supported some impressively thorough (and readable) biographies. An example is Elizabeth Longford's *A Pilgrimage of Passion: The Life of Wilfrid Scawen Blunt* (New York: Knopf, 1980). The late Lady Longford was one of the most prolific biographers of Victorian subjects. Among the fifty or so biographies of T. E. Lawrence, the most important landmarks are the passionately hostile assault by Richard Aldington, *Lawrence of Arabia: A Biographical Inquiry* (New York: Greenwood Press, 1976); the psychobiography by John E. Mack, *A Prince of Our Disorder: The Life of T. E. Lawrence* (Boston: Little, Brown, 1978); and the massive narrative by Jeremy Wilson, *Lawrence of Arabia: The Authorized Biography of T. E. Lawrence* (New York: Atheneum, 1990), which is meant to save Lawrence from the debunkers and psychologizers. These should be read in conjunction with Elie Kedourie's "Colonel Lawrence and His Biographers," in Kedourie's *Islam and the Modern World* (New York: Holt, Rinehart and Winston, 1981), 261–75—largely a refutation of Mack's work. Another landmark biography is Elizabeth Monroe's *Philby of Arabia* (London: Faber and Faber, 1973). H. V. F. Winstone has made the biography of the English among the Arabs into his special trade, by writing *Captain Shakespear: A Portrait* (New York: Quartet Books, 1978), *Gertrude Bell* (New York: Quartet Books, 1978), and *Leachman: "OC Desert": The Life of Lieutenant-Colonel Gerard Leachman D.S.O.* (New York: Quartet Books, 1982). The reader will also find many subtle sketches of the English in the Middle East; among the most evocative are Albert Hourani's essays on Wilfrid Scawen Blunt and H. A. R. Gibb, in his *Europe and the Middle East* (Berkeley and Los Angeles: University of California Press, 1980).

Not to be overlooked are the many biographies of Zionist leaders, who left behind vast collections of intimate materials that have inspired several modern, thoroughly documented biographies. On Theodor Herzl are the studies by Amos Elon, *Herzl* (New York: Schocken Books, 1986), and by Ernst Pawel, *The Labyrinth of Exile: A Life of Theodor Herzl* (New York: Farrar, Straus and Giroux, 1989). These may be supplemented with the provocative sketch by Peter Loewenberg, "Theodor Herzl: Nationalism and Politics," in his *Decoding the Past: The Psychohistorical Approach* (Berkeley and Los Angeles: University of California Press, 1985), 101–35. So rich is the documentation for the lives of many Zionist leaders that many of their biographers have produced multivolume works. Particularly noteworthy are the first volumes published by Jehuda Reinharz, *Chaim Weizmann: The Making of a Zionist Leader* (New York: Oxford University Press, 1985), and by Shabtai Teveth, *Ben-Gurion: The Burning Ground, 1886–1948* (Boston: Houghton Mifflin, 1987). Additional volumes will follow. Anita Shapira's *Berl: The Biography of a Socialist Zionist* (Cambridge: Cambridge University Press, 1985) is an English distillation of a larger multivolume biography in Hebrew, and an example of the full potential of intellectual biography. And on and on, ad (almost) infinitum.

Notes
Contributors
Index

Notes

Introduction

1. See Maxime Rodinson, "A Critical Survey of Modern Studies on Muhammad," in *Studies on Islam,* ed. and trans. Merlin L. Swartz (New York: Oxford University Press, 1981), 23–85.

2. Hamilton A. R. Gibb, "Problems of Modern Middle Eastern History," in *Studies on the Civilization of Islam,* ed. Stanford J. Shaw and William R. Polk (1956; Boston: Beacon, 1962), 340–41.

3. Albert Hourani, "The Present State of Islamic and Middle Eastern Historiography," in *Europe and the Middle East* (Berkeley and Los Angeles: University of California Press, 1980), 163, 191.

4. Peter Gran, "Political Economy as a Paradigm for the Study of Islamic History," *International Journal of Middle Eastern Studies* 11 (1980): 512.

5. Gertrude Himmelfarb, "Some Reflections on the New History," *American Historical Review* 94, no. 3 (June 1989): 662.

6. Malcolm Yapp, "More Enigma Than Statesman" (review article including Patrick Seale, *Asad: The Struggle for Syria,* and Moshe Ma'oz, *Asad: The Sphinx of Damascus*), *Times Literary Supplement,* November 4–10, 1988.

2. Traditional Islamic Learning and Ideas of the Person in the Twentieth Century

Arabic names and terms are transliterated from classical or spoken Arabic according to context. The author thanks Deborah Hodges for comments on this essay.

1. L. Carl Brown, *The Tunisia of Ahmad Bey, 1837–1855* (Princeton: Princeton University Press, 1974), 161. See also E. Lévy-Provençal, *Les historiens des chorfa* (Paris: Librairie Orientaliste Paul

Geuthner, 1922), 11; and Abdallah Laroui, *L'idéologie arabe contemporaine* (Paris: François Maspéro, 1967), 19–28.

2. The analogy of the Iranian clerics to Ronald Reagan is Yann Richard's (personal communication, June 2, 1987). For Egypt, see Gilles Kepel, *Muslim Extremism in Egypt: The Prophet and Pharaoh*, trans. Jon Rothschild (Berkeley and Los Angeles: University of California Press, 1986), 99–101, 173. See also Dale F. Eickelman, "National Identity and Religious Discourse in Contemporary Oman," *International Journal of Islamic and Arabic Studies* 6 (1989): pp. 1–20.

3. See Allan Christelow, *Muslim Law Courts and the French Colonial State in Algeria* (Princeton: Princeton University Press, 1985), 110. For an authoritative survey of ulama throughout the Maghrib, see Pessah Shinar, " 'Ulamaʾ, Marabouts and Government: An Overview of Their Relationships in the French Colonial Maghrib," in *Religion and Government in the World of Islam*, ed. Joel L. Kraemer and Ilai Alon, *Israel Oriental Studies*, vol. 10 (Tel Aviv: Tel Aviv University, 1980), 211–29.

4. See Dale F. Eickelman, "Religion in Polity and Society," in *The Political Economy of Morocco*, ed. I. William Zartman (New York: Praeger, 1987), 84–97.

5. Three manuscripts by al-Thaʿalibi (A.D. 961–1038), *Tarjama al-Shuʿaraʾ*, *Tarjama al-katib fi adab al-sahib*, and *Tarjama al-Muttanabi*, use the term in their titles, whereas al-Yaqut's (d. A.D. 1229) *Muʿjam al-Udabaʾ*, ed. D. S. Margoliouth (Cairo: Dar Ihyaʾ al-turath al-ʿArabi, 1936), 26–27, refers to scholars prior to himself, such as Abu ʿAbbas ibn Yahya al-Shaybani, whose writings date from the ninth century. I am grateful to Adel Sulaiman Gamal of the University of Arizona for bringing these references to my attention.

6. See Dale F. Eickelman, *Knowledge and Power in Morocco: The Education of a Twentieth-Century Notable* (Princeton: Princeton University Press, 1985), 59–65; and Dale F. Eickelman, "Religious Knowledge in Inner Oman," *Journal of Oman Studies* 6 (1983): 166–67. On the association of literacy with other attributes of high status in the Yemen, see Brinkley Messick, "Legal Documents and the Concept of 'Restricted Literacy' in a Traditional Society," *International Journal of the Sociology of Language* 42 (1983): 43–44.

7. J. S. La Fontaine, "Person and Individual: Some Anthropolog-

ical Reflections," in *The Category of the Person,* ed. Michael Carrithers, Steven Collins, and Steven Lukes (Cambridge: Cambridge University Press, 1985), 124, 126, 133.

8. Marcel Mauss, "A Category of the Human Mind: The Notion of Person; The Notion of Self" (orig. 1938), in ibid., 14.

9. Ibid., 13–14, 18–32.

10. Abu Ja'far Muhammad ibn Jarir al-Tabari, *Ta'rikh,* ed. Muhammad Abu Fadil Ibrahim (Cairo: Dar al-Ma'arif, 1964), 1937.

11. Mukhtar al-Susi's *al-Ma'sul* (Casablanca: al-Najah Press, 1961), a compendium of tarjamas, contains numerous entries that cumulatively suggest that many men of learning come from households in which the father or another close relative is literate and takes an active role in encouraging Qur'anic recitation.

12. On genealogical representations of self, see Abdelahad Sebti, "Au Maroc: Sharifisme citadin, charisme et historiographie," *Annales: Économies, Sociétés, Civilisations* 41, no. 2 (March–April 1986): 433–57; the cited "modern" autobiographies are Taha Hussein, *The Stream of Days,* trans. Hilary Waymont (London: Longmans, Green, and Co., 1948); and Malek Bennabi, *Mémoires d'un témoin du siècle* (Algiers: Éditions Nationales Algériennes, 1965).

13. For example, 'Allal al-Fasi, *al-Naqd al-dhati,* 5th ed. (1952; Rabat: al-Risala Press, 1979).

14. Consider, for example, the profile of Palestinian religious activists offered by Jean-François Legrain, in "Islamites et lutte nationale Palestinienne dans les territoires occupés par Israël," *Revue Français de Science Politique* 36, no. 2 (April 1986): 241–43—young and well-educated compared to the general population, deprived of all hope of "social integration," and often rural in origin. Despite the religious commitment of activists, their pamphlets and slogans rarely cite the Qur'an or *hadith* literature.

15. Ahmad Mansuri's tarjama was written between 1962 and 1963 at the request of a schoolteacher assigned to Bzu. The teacher came from Tetouan, the former capital of Morocco's Spanish zone, and became interested in local history. 'Abd al-Rahman Mansuri's tarjama was prepared at my request in 1976. It is a short document of two pages, brief in part because of extensive interviews carried out over several years and described at length in Eickelman, *Knowledge and Power in Morocco.* Ahmad al-Bu 'Ayyashi's tarjama, a document of six single-spaced pages in Arabic, was written in 1976.

16. Interview, northern Oman, June 8, 1980.

17. "Kitab tabsirat al-muʿtabirin fi taʾrikh al-ʿAbriyin" [Book for the enlightenment of passers-by on the history of the ʿAbriyin]. The manuscript is undated but from internal evidence was composed between 1956 and 1958–59. The first page of the manuscript states: "Copy finished 1378 [A.D. 1958–59] by Saʿid bin ʿAbd Allah bin Muhammad al-Daghghari, by order of Shaykh Muhammad bin Amir." The manuscript is in the possession of Jabir Musa al-ʿAbri, Nizwa.

18. On several occasions in 1979 and 1980, and again in 1982, I saw Shaykh Ibrahim's manuscript and similar ones being publicly read by men of learning. These readings took place in tribal guest houses, with other men of learning present, in addition to tribespeople and other interested onlookers. Occasionally particular points in the manuscript were clarified or discussed among senior participants.

19. For example, *shurafaʾ*, recognized descendants of the Prophet Muhammad through his daughter Fatima, were exempt from taxation and from corvée labor, among other privileges, prior to the protectorate.

20. One of these is the support of his father and tribe for ʿAbd al-Krim al-Khattabi, who was a qadi in Spanish Melilla prior to his revolt, and thus in a role not dissimilar to that of Bu ʿAyyashi. It is interesting that of Bu ʿAyyashi's personally established ties with the nationalists, he emphasizes those with leaders in former French Morocco instead of the former Spanish zone, where he spent all of his career after 1937. Although his sentiments are undoubtedly nationalistic, it is possible that his persona as a Muslim nationalist was better supported by claims to linkages less susceptible to verification in the northern zone itself. For an example of the biography of an early-twentieth-century Moroccan man of learning that also skillfully bridges the divide between nationalism and reformism within the format of the tarjama, see ʿAbd Allah Jirari, *al-Muhaddith al-hafiz Abu Shuʿayb al-Dukkali* (Jadida and Casablanca: al-Najah Press, 1976), one of a series of books in a similar format on "Moroccan Personalities." The series itself suggests that the tarjama as a literary form still commands a significant audience in Morocco.

3. Autobiography and Biography in the Middle East:
A Plea for Psychopolitical Studies

The author wishes to thank Mr. Cyrus Amir-Mokri of the Department of History of the University of Chicago for his valuable assistance in the preparation of this paper. Mrs. Layla Kassem of the Committee on Human Development of the university was also helpful.

1. Karl J. Weintraub, "Autobiography and Historical Consciousness," *Critical Inquiry* 1, no. 4 (1974–75): 824.

2. Ibid., 821–22.

3. In referring to the Middle East, this author means to include the Arabic-speaking states, Turkey, and Iran. Israel is specifically excluded, not because it is not part of the Middle East in a geographical or political sense, but because it is not considered a part of the Middle East in a cultural sense in terms of the central themes of this paper. Clearly, this geographical construct is of limited utility. It is posed at a level of abstraction that is so great as to nearly vitiate its utility—nearly, but not entirely. Appreciating the level of abstraction, one can still, as argued here, produce useful generalization. The same is true for the construct of the West.

Equally adamant disclaimers have to be made for the use of the generalization "culture" when speaking of the Middle East. There is no single Middle Eastern culture—whether Israel is or is not considered part of the region—but three principal cultural arenas in addition to the culture(s) of the state of Israel. Each of these major cultures is unified only at a particular level of abstraction that may not be useful for scholarly purposes. There are also countless minor cultures that are not part of the four major cultures of the region.

For the purposes of this paper, "culture" will be used to refer to the aggregated cultures of the Persian-, Turkish-, and Arabic-speaking areas of the Middle East. The reader must appreciate the author's serious reservations about the meaningfulness of the construct, while appreciating the efficiencies in writing that can nonetheless be achieved by retaining the concept.

4. Literary works from the region that appear to adhere more closely to Weintraub's criteria for "true autobiography" than do most other Middle Eastern examples include the following: In Arabic, Ah-

mad Amin, *Hayati* (Cairo: Maktabat al-Nahdah al-Misriyah, 1961); ʿAbd al-ʿAziz Fahmi, *Hadhihi Hayati* (Cairo: Dar al-Hilal, 1963); Taha Husayn, *al-Ayyam,* 2 vols. (Cairo: Dar al-Maʿarif, 1966); and Ahmad Lufti al-Sayyid, *Qissat Hayat* (Cairo: Dar al-Hilal, 1962). For a general introduction to this genre in Arabic, see ʿAli ʿAbduh Barakat, *Iʿtirafat Udabaʾina fi Siyarihim al-Dhatiyah* (Jidda: Tihama Publications, 1982). In Persian, Qasim Ghani, *Yadʾdashtʾha-yi Duktur Qasim-i Ghani,* vol. 1 (London: Cyrus Ghani, distributed by Ithaca Press, 1980); Muhammad ʿAli Jamalzadeh, *Isfahan Is Half the World: Memories of a Persian Boyhood,* trans. W. L. Heston (Princeton: Princeton University Press, 1983); and Ahmad Kasravi, *Zindigani-i Man* (Tehran: Jar, 1976). Included with these works must be the following, of a somewhat different order: Mohammad Reza Shah, *Mission For My Country* (New York: McGraw-Hill, 1961); and Ashraf Pahlavi, *Faces in a Mirror: Memoirs from Exile* (Englewood Cliffs, N.J.: Prentice Hall, 1980). In Turkish, Halide Edibe Adivar, *Memoirs of Halide Edibe* (New York: Arno Press, 1972); and Reşat Nuri Güntekin, *The Autobiography of a Turkish Girl,* trans. Wyndham Deedes (London: Allen and Unwin, 1949).

5. There are, of course, some. For Persian biographies, see, for example, Nasrullah Falsafi, *Zindigani-i Shah ʿAbbas-i Avval,* 4 vols. (Tehran: Kitab-i Kayhan, 1962); Muhammad Husayn Maymadiʾnizhad, *Zindigi-i Pur Majara-i Nader Shah* (Tehran: Saziman-i Intisharat-i Javidan, 1966); Abdul Husayn Navaʾi, *Sharh-i Hal-i ʿAbbas Mirza Mulkʾara* (Tehran: Intisharat-i Babak, 1976); Akbar-i Hashemi-i Rafsanjani, *Amir Kabir Ya Qahriman-i Mubarizeh Ba Istiʿmar* (Tehran: Muʾasisehʾi Matbuʿati-i Faranahi, 1967); Ismaʿil Raʾin, *Haydar Khan ʿAmu Ghuli* (Tehran: Saziman-i Intisharat-i Javidan, 1973); Ismaʿil Raʾin, *Mirza Malkum Khan* (Tehran: Bungah-i Matbuʿati-i Safi ʿAli Shah, 1971); and Rahimzadeh-i Safavi, *Zindigani-i Shah Ismaʿil-i Safavi* (Tehran: Ketab Forushi-i Khayyam, 1961).

6. Weintraub, "Autobiography and Historical Consciousness," 821.

7. Abdallah Laroui, *The Crisis of the Arab Intellectual: Traditionalism or Historicism?* (Berkeley and Los Angeles: University of California Press, 1976).

8. Weintraub, "Autobiography and Historical Consciousness," 826.

9. These works are Fouad Ajami, *The Vanished Imam: Musa al Sadr and the Shia of Lebanon* (Ithaca: Cornell University Press, 1986); Vincent Crapanzano, *Tuhami: Portrait of a Moroccan* (Chicago: University of Chicago Press, 1980); Roy Mottahedeh, *The Mantle of the Prophet: Religion and Politics in Iran* (New York: Simon and Schuster, 1985); and Vamik D. Volkan and Norman Itzkowitz, *The Immortal Atatürk: A Psychobiography* (Chicago: University of Chicago Press, 1984).

10. Crapanzano, *Tuhami*, 136.

11. Ibid., 7.

12. Ibid., 124.

13. Weintraub, "Autobiography and Historical Consciousness," 824.

14. I have referred to this enterprise as "psychopolitical studies" because the term captures the nature of the effort to use psychology to understand political phenomena. For the reasons suggested, psychobiography is inadequate, but so are psychohistory and psychosocial studies, since both of the latter fail to specify the domain of inquiry as political. As infelicitous as the term psychopolitical studies is, it appears to best capture the nature of the intellectual enterprise here being advocated.

15. Marvin Zonis, *Majestic Failure: The Fall of the Shah of Iran* (Chicago: University of Chicago Press, 1991). It is recognized that a variety of other, equally legitimate studies of the revolution could have been done. Almost nothing has been written, for example, from the point of view of the winners: nothing about the organization of the principal actors in the victorious coalition, their financing, and the precise leadership role of Ayatollah Khomeini and others. In addition, a study of the revolution could usefully adopt a more explicitly group focus.

16. This is not the place for a detailed explanation of how the character structure of the Shah and the steps he took to provide himself with narcissistic supplies significantly helped to produce the rage of the Iranian people that fed the revolution. But by the 1970s, the Iranian people appear to have become ever less tolerant of the Shah's ever increasing efforts to sustain his narcissistic balance. One such effort—his grandiosity and all that flowed from it—was especially offensive to them.

17. One unconventional distinction between the physical and the social sciences, that concerning the role of prediction, may disappear with a new formulation of the physical sciences, a formulation based on the study of nonlinearity. For a description of nonlinearity, see Frank M. Richter, "Nonlinear Behavior," in *Metatheory in Social Science,* ed. Donald W. Fiske and Richard A. Shweder (Chicago: University of Chicago Press, 1986). For a description of the "new science" see James Gleick, *Chaos, Making a New Science* (New York: Viking, 1987).

18. William M. Runyan, *Life Histories and Psychobiography: Explorations in Theory and Method* (New York: Oxford University Press, 1982), 127.

19. Ibid., quoting here from D. B. Bromley.

20. Hans-Georg Gadamer, "The Problem of Historical Consciousness," in *Interpretive Social Sciences: A Reader,* ed. P. Rabinow and W. Sullivan (Berkeley and Los Angeles: University of California Press, 1979), 116 (emphasis in the original). What precisely Gadamer means to suggest by the use of "true" is puzzling in this context.

21. See the brilliant study of terrorism by Richard E. Rubenstein, *Alchemists of the Revolution: Terrorism in the Modern World* (New York: Basic Books, 1987).

22. See the important psychopolitical study by the Committee on International Relations, *Self-Involvement in the Middle East Crisis,* vol. 10, no. 103 (New York: Group for the Advancement of Psychiatry, November 1978).

23. Crapanzano, *Tuhami,* 130.

24. Runyan, *Life Histories,* 150.

25. Peter Winch, "Understanding a Primitive Society," *American Philosophical Quarterly* 1 (1964): 307–24, passim; E. D. Hirsch, "Old and New in Hermeneutics," in his *The Aims of Interpretation* (Chicago: University of Chicago Press, 1978), 33.

26. For an article that argues the similarity of problems of interpretation and thus validity in the natural sciences and hermeneutics, see Mary Hesse, "In Defence of Objectivity," *Proceedings of the British Academy* 68 (1972): 275–92.

27. Roy Schafer, "Narration in Psychoanalytic Dialogue," *Critical Inquiry* 7 (Autumn 1980): 30. For a fascinating argument that another source of the "assumptions" is the language itself, see Hayden

White, *Metahistory: The Historical Imagination in Nineteenth Century Europe* (Baltimore: Johns Hopkins University Press, 1973), especially the section "Poetics and History." If White is correct (and he presents a compelling argument), then the difficulties of cross-cultural investigations are greater than we had previously imagined.

28. Donald Polkinghorne, *Methodology for the Human Sciences* (Albany: State University of New York Press, 1983), 241.

4. Biography and Psychohistory

1. Carlo Antoni, *From History to Sociology,* trans. Hayden V. White (Detroit: Wayne State University Press, 1959).

5. A Response to Critics of a Psychobiography

1. Vamik D. Volkan and Norman Itzkowitz, *The Immortal Atatürk: A Psychobiography* (Chicago: University of Chicago Press, 1984).

2. Vamik D. Volkan, "Problems of Methodology in Psychoanalytic Biography" (Paper presented at panel, "Freud's Vision: Key Issues in the Methodology of Applied Psychoanalysis," fall meeting of the American Psychoanalytic Association, New York, December 1986).

3. William G. Niederland, "The Naming of America," in *The Unconscious Today: Essays in Honor of Max Schur,* ed. M. Kanzer (New York: International Universities Press, 1971), 459–72.

4. Peter Gay, *Freud, A Life for Our Time* (New York: Norton, 1988).

5. Sigmund Freud, *Leonardo da Vinci and a Memory of His Childhood,* in *Standard Edition,* vol. 11 (1910; London: Hogarth Press, 1967), 130.

6. Vamik D. Volkan, *The Need to Have Enemies and Allies: From Clinical Practice to International Relations* (Northvale, N.J.: Jason Aronson, 1988).

7. Vamik D. Volkan, "Narcissistic Personality Organization and 'Reparative' Leadership," *International Journal of Group Psychotherapy* 30 (1980): 131–52; Volkan and Itzkowitz, *The Immortal Atatürk.*

8. See Erik Erikson, *Young Man Luther* (New York: Norton,

1958); J. E. Gedo, "The Methodology of Psychoanalytic Biography," *Journal of the American Psychoanalytic Association* 20 (1972): 638–49; J. E. Mack, "Psychoanalysis and Historical Biography," *Journal of the American Psychoanalytic Association* 19 (1971): 143–79.

9. A. Falk, "Aspects of Political Psychobiography," *Political Psychology* 6 (1985): 605–19.

10. Ives Hendrick, *Facts and Theories of Psychoanalysis* (New York: Knopf, 1950).

11. Vamik D. Volkan, *What Do You Get When You Cross a Dandelion with a Rose? The True Story of a Psychoanalysis* (New York: Jason Aronson, 1984); Vamik D. Volkan, *Six Steps in the Treatment of Borderline Personality Organization* (Northvale, N.J.: Jason Aronson, 1987).

12. Sigmund Freud, *Fragments of an Analysis of a Case of Hysteria,* in *Standard Edition,* vol. 7 (1905; London: Hogarth Press, 1953), 3–122.

13. Harry Stack Sullivan, *The Interpersonal Theory of Psychiatry* (1946–47; New York: Norton, 1953); David Rapaport, "The Structure of Psychoanalytic Theory: A Systematizing Attempt," in *Psychological Issues,* vol. 2, monograph 6 (New York: International Universities Press, 1960).

14. Rapaport, "The Structure of Psychoanalytic Theory."

15. Sigmund Freud, *The Interpretation of Dreams,* in *Standard Edition,* vols. 4 and 5 (1900; London: Hogarth Press, 1961).

16. Phyllis Greenacre, Swift and Carroll: A Psychoanalytic Study of Two Lives (New York: International Universities Press, 1955); M. S. Bergmann, "Limitations of Method in Psychoanalytic Biography: A Historical Inquiry," *Journal of the American Psychoanalytic Association* 21 (1973): 833–50.

17. William G. Niederland, "An Analytic Inquiry into the Life and Work of Heinrich Schliemann," in *Drives, Affects, Behavior,* vol. 2, ed. M. Schur (New York: International Universities Press, 1965).

18. Kemal H. Karpat, "Review Article: The Personality of Atatürk," *American Historical Review* 90 (1985): 893–99.

19. Mack, "Psychoanalysis and Historical Biography"; Falk, "Aspects of Political Psychobiography"; Peter Loewenberg, "Historical Method, the Subjectivity of the Researcher, and Psychohistory," in *Rapports,* vol. 2, *Psychohistory: A Frontier in Method* (Stuttgart: Comité International des Sciences Historiques, 1985).

6. History versus Biography

1. See Shabtai Teveth, *Ben-Gurion: The Burning Ground, 1886–1948* (Boston: Houghton Mifflin, 1987). Numerous discussions and quotes throughout the remainder of this essay are from this biography.

7. The Biographical Element in Political History

1. James William Anderson, "The Methodology of Psychological Biography," *Journal of Interdisciplinary History* 11, no. 3 (Winter 1981): 455–75.

2. Uriel Dann, *Iraq under Qassem: A Political History, 1958–1963* (New York: Praeger, 1969), 78–79.

3. E. W. Polson Newman, *The Middle East* (London: Geoffrey Bles, 1926), after 272.

Contributors

URIEL DANN is Professor of History Emeritus at Tel Aviv University. He is the author of *Iraq under Qassem, Studies in the History of Transjordan,* and *King Hussein and the Challenge of Arab Radicalism.*

DALE F. EICKELMAN is Lazarus Professor of Anthropology and Human Relations at Dartmouth College. He is the author of *Moroccan Islam: Tradition and Society in a Pilgrimage Center, The Middle East: An Anthropological Approach,* and *Knowledge and Power in Morocco: The Education of a Twentieth-Century Notable.*

NORMAN ITZKOWITZ is Professor of Near Eastern Studies at Princeton University and has trained with the National Psychological Association for Psychoanalysis. His books include *Ottoman Empire and Islamic Tradition* and (with Vamik D. Volkan) *The Immortal Atatürk: A Psychobiography.*

ELIE KEDOURIE is Professor of Politics Emeritus at the University of London and Fellow of the British Academy. He is the editor of the quarterly *Middle Eastern Studies* and the author of many books on the political history of the Middle East. His most recent are *Arabic Political Memoirs, In the Anglo-Arab Labyrinth, Islam in the Modern World,* and *The Crossman Confessions.*

MARTIN KRAMER, the volume editor, is Associate Director of the Moshe Dayan Center for Middle Eastern and African Studies at Tel Aviv University. He is the author of *Islam Assembled.*

BERNARD LEWIS is Cleveland E. Dodge Professor of Near Eastern Studies Emeritus at Princeton University. His most recent books include *The Muslim Discovery of Europe, The Jews of Islam, The Political Language of Islam,* and *Race and Slavery in the Middle East.*

SHABTAI TEVETH is the author of a multivolume biography of David Ben-Gurion, of which three volumes have been published in Hebrew. His published books in English include *Moshe Dayan: A Biography, Ben-Gurion and the Palestinian Arabs,* and *Ben-Gurion: The Burning Ground, 1886–1948.*

VAMIK D. VOLKAN, M.D., is a psychoanalyst of Cypriot Turkish origin and Professor of Psychiatry at the University of Virginia School of Medicine. His numerous books include *Cyprus—War and Adaptation: A Psychoanalytic History* and (with Norman Itzkowitz) *The Immortal Atatürk: A Psychobiography.*

MARVIN ZONIS is Professor in the Graduate School of Business at the University of Chicago. He is author of *The Political Elite of Iran* and *Majestic Failure: The Fall of the Shah of Iran.*

Index

'Abbas Hilmi, 132
Abbasids, 94
'Abd al-Krim al-Khattabi, 45, 150n20
'Abdallah, king of Transjordan, 118,
    120, 125, 134, 139
'Abdin Palace, 123
'Abduh, Muhammad, 130
Abdülhamid II, 9, 20, 131–32
al-'Abri, Ibrahim Sa'id, 52–55
'Abriyin, 52
Abu Dhabi, 49
Abu Iyad, 139
Abu Nidal, 135
Adams, Charles, 94
Adler, Alfred, 85, 95
al-Afghani, Jamal al-Din, 8–9, 94, 128
Ahmad Bey, 131
Ait 'Tab, 43
Ait Waryaghar, *see* Bani Waryajil
Ajami, Fouad, 65–67, 134
Alam, Assadollah, 73
Aldington, Richard, 141
Algar, Hamid, 128, 137–38
Algeria, 36, 40
Ali, Muhammad, 131
'alim, see ulama
Amanat, Abbas, 132
Amenemhet, 21
Ames, Robert, 80
Amin, Ahmad, 130
Amman, 125
Anatolia, 98–99, 102
Angola, 116
Ankara, 99
Annales school, 5–6, 94
anthropology, 14, 118, 139–40
Antoni, Carlo, 95

Antonius, George, 129
Arabia, 24, 33, 38. *See also* Oman;
    Saudi Arabia
Arabs, *see individual countries*
Arafat, Yasir, 135
Armenians, 101–2
Arnold, Matthew, 100
Arslan, Shakib, 129
Arutin, 31
al-Asad, Hafiz, 134
Assyria, 22
Atatürk, Mustafa Kemal, 16, 66–68,
    97–103, 106–8, 136–37
Atlas Mountains, 42
Augustine, 1, 91
Augustus, 93
Austria, 32
autobibliography, 29–30
autobiography and self-narrative (as
    literary forms), 2–3, 13–14, 19,
    21–26, 29, 31–34, 36, 39–41, 60–
    65, 68, 125; bibliography of, 130,
    138–40, 151n4, 152n5; and dia-
    ries, 2, 7–8, 10, 45, 60, 62, 105,
    115, 141; and memoirs, 3, 20–21,
    23–25, 28, 30–34, 40, 60, 62, 125,
    138–40; and tarjamas, 14–15, 36,
    39–47, 52–59, 149n15, 150n20;
    and travel, travelogues, 24, 26–28,
    31–33, 62, 141. *See also* sources
Avicenna, 34
Ayyam al-'Arab, 24
al-Ayyam (Stream of Days), 130
'Ayyash, 46
'Ayyashi, Ahmad bin 'Abd al-Salam al-
    Bu, 42, 45–48, 57, 149n15,
    150n20

161

Azilal, 43–44
Aztecs, 93
Azulay, 31

Babar, 25
Babinger, Franz, 131
Baghdad, 9, 94, 120, 133
Bahla, 53–54
Baluch, 49
Bani Waryajil, 45–47
Baqir al-Sadr, Muhammad, 50
al-Barq al-Shami, 25, 32
Bashir, Suleyman, 94
Batatu, Hanna, 123
Baz, Rustum, 31
Beeson, Irene, 136
Beethoven, 110–11
Behistun inscription, 22
Beirut, 80
Ben-Ami, Shlomo, 122
Ben-Gurion, David, 18, 109–11, 113–17, 143
Bennabi, Malek, 40
Berber, 24, 42, 46
Bible, 22, 90
biography (as a literary form), 2–19, 25, 28, 30, 32, 36, 39–40, 55, 60–68, 75, 89–90, 93–98, 101, 103–13, 118–22, 125; bibliography of, 127–38, 141–43; relation to history and historiography, 2–7, 17–19, 62–63, 89–96, 100–101, 107, 109–13, 118–26. See also psycho-biography; sources
Birdwood, Lord, 133
Blake, Robert, 119
Bloomsbury, 8
Blunt, Wilfred Scawen, 141–42
Boujad, 45
Bradford, Selina, countess of, 119
Braudel, Fernand, 94
Brecht, Bertolt, 112
Britain, British, 5, 17, 116, 119–21, 125, 141–42
Brown, L. Carl, 35, 131
Browne, Edward G., 94
Buckle, George Earl, 89

Buckley, William, 80
Burzoye, 24
Buyids, 29
Bzu, 42–45

Caesar, Julius, 30, 110–11
Cairo, 8, 29–30
Carter, Jimmy, 71, 74, 80
Casey, William J., 80
Caspian Sea, 72
censorship, 8, 123
Chamberlain, Neville, 111
Champollion, Jean François, 93
charisma, 11, 102, 121, 128
Chelebi, Evliya, 27
childhood, children, 28, 40, 70–71, 75, 95, 101, 105, 107, 125, 130, 140
China, 26, 38, 70
Christianity, Christians, 1, 38, 90
Churchill, Winston, 71, 110
CIA, 71, 80–81
Cicero, 93
communalism, 14
Constantinople, see Istanbul
Contras, see Iran-Contra affair
Cox, Henry, 125
Crapanzano, Vincent, 65–67, 83, 140
Critchfield, Richard, 140
Crusades, 25
Cyprus, 97

Damascus, 8–9, 133–34
Dann, Uriel, 18, 133
Darius, 22
daʿwa (Fatimid), 29
deconstructionism, 6
De Gaulle, Charles, 31
de Gaury, Gerald, 135
determinism, 16, 99
Deuteronomy, Book of, 22
Dhufar, 48–49
diaries, see autobiography
Diba, Farhad, 137
dictionaries, biographical, 28, 30, 55, 89, 138
Dilthey, Wilhelm, 93

Disraeli, Benjamin, 89, 94, 119
Dubai, 49
Eden, Anthony, 9
Egypt, Egyptians, 9, 21, 26, 28, 32,
    40, 121, 123, 129–32, 136, 140
Eickelman, Dale F., 13–15, 139
Elizabeth I, 110
Elon, Amos, 142
Erikson, Erik, 103
Essex, Robert Devereux, earl of, 110
Evian Conference, 116
Falk, Avner, 103, 108
family relations, 11, 14, 22, 31, 39–
    40, 50, 56, 105, 125, 132–33. See
    also childhood; women
Faruq I, 136
al-Fasi, ʿAllal, 40–41
Fatimids, 26, 29–30
Faysal, king of Iraq, 9, 133
Faysal, king of Saudi Arabia, 135
Fez, 40, 46–47
Fischer, Michael M. J., 138
Forrestal, James V., 96
France, French, 5–6, 8, 14, 22, 130;
    rule in Morocco, 43–46, 56–57
Frederick the Great, 121
Freud, Sigmund, 85–87, 95, 98–101,
    103–4, 106
Friedländer, Saul, 17

Gadamer, Hans-Georg, 79
Gay, Peter, 99
Gaza, 123
Gendzier, Irene, 129
genealogy, 22–23, 31, 33, 41–43, 45–
    46, 53
Geneva, 129
Germany, Germans, 91, 116–17, 122
Ghazali, 1, 29, 34
Gibb, Hamilton, 5, 142
Gibbon, Edward, 126
Gilbert, William, 112
Glaser, Edward, 32
Gökalp, Ziya, 129
Goldziher, Ignaz, 93

Greece, Greeks, 22–23, 33, 102
Güntekin, Reşat Nuri, 140
Guyana, 116

Habshush, Hayyim, 32
Hadani, Eldad, 31
hadith, 26, 33, 93
Hadramawt, 48
hagiography, 1–2, 29, 40, 54, 56
Haifa, 115
Halévy, Joseph, 32
Hallaj, 5, 29
Hamraʾ al-ʿAbriyin, 51
Hanover, 121
Hart, Alan, 135
Harun ibn Yahya, 27
Hashemi, Ali, 139
Hashemites, 125, 133, 139
Haslip, Joan, 132
Hatusilis, 21
Haykal, Muhammad Husayn, 129
Hegel, Wilhelm Friedrich, 92
hero, concept of, 11, 18, 101–2, 119–
    21, 128, 135
Herzl, Theodor, 9, 142
Heyd, Uriel, 129
Hijaz, 26
Hindus, 48
Hirsch, E. D., 84
Hirst, David, 136
historicism, 13, 61–63, 91
historism, 61, 91
history, see biography
Hitler, Adolf, 102, 111, 114–17, 121
Hittites, 21–22
Holocaust, 116–17
homosexuality, 128
Hormuz, 49
Hourani, Albert, 5, 127, 130, 142
Howarth, David, 135
Hunayn ibn Ishaq, 28
Hungary, 32
Husayn, king of Jordan, 118, 120,
    124–25, 134, 139
Husayn, sharif of Mecca, 133
Husayn, Saddam, 121, 133
Husayn, Taha, 40, 130

al-Husayni, Muhammad Amin, 134
al-Husri, Sati', 129

Ibadiyya, 48, 50, 52, 54
Ibn Abi Usaybi'a, 28
Ibn Battuta, 27
Ibn Buluggin, 'Abdallah, 24
Ibn Hisham, 94
Ibn Khaldun, 31
Ibn Miskawayh, 23
Ibn Qays, 'Azzan, 53
Ibn Ridwan, 28
Ibn Sa'ud, 'Abd al-'Aziz, 9, 46, 135
Ibn Tulun, 31
Ifham al-Yahud, 31
'Imad al-Din, 25
imamate (Oman), 15, 48, 51–54
India, 24, 27, 38, 49
intellectuals, intelligentsia, 8, 35, 63,
    66, 127–30. *See also* ulama
interviews, *see* sources
Iran, Iranians, 9, 15, 22–25, 27, 35,
    49, 66, 69–76, 79–82, 123, 128,
    132, 137, 139–40, 153n15
Iran-Contra affair, 79, 81–82
Iraq, Iraqis, 12, 29, 50, 81, 116, 118,
    121, 123, 125, 133
Isfahan, 140
Islam, 1–4, 13–14, 20, 23–38, 55–58,
    89–90, 128; and concept of indi-
    vidual, 1–5, 12–14, 37–40, 61–63,
    89–90
Islamic Jihad, 80
Isma'il, khedive of Egypt, 132
Ismail Kemal Bey, 138–39
Ismailis, 29
Israel, Israelis, 17, 82, 110, 117, 123,
    124, 151n3. *See also* Zionism
Israeli, Raphael, 136
Istanbul, 8, 27, 98–99
Itzkowitz, Norman, 16–17, 65–67,
    137

Jaffa, 115
Jamal Pasha, 139
Jamalzadeh, Muhammad 'Ali, 140
Jerusalem, 31, 123, 134

Jesus, 1
Jews, 22–23, 31–32, 90, 111, 113–
    17, 123. *See also* Israel; Zionism
Jordan, Jordanians, 12, 116, 118,
    121, 123, 125, 133–34, 139
Josephus, 22–23, 33
journalists (as biographers), 9, 132–
    34, 136, 139–40
Jung, Carl, 85, 95

Kalila wa-Dimna, 24
Kamaliyin, 49
Kâmil Pasha, 20
Karpat, Kemal, 107
Keddie, Nikki, 128
Kedourie, Elie, 16–17, 142
Kellerman, Barbara, 138
Khadduri, Majid, 138
al-Khalili, Muhammad ibn 'Abdallah,
    52
Khassab, 49
Khayat, As'ad, 33
Khayr al-Din al-Tunisi, 33
Khomeini, Rouhollah, 35, 69, 137–
    38, 153n15
Khusraw Anushirvan, 23
Khusru Parviz, 23
Kibrisli Mehmet Pasha, Mme., 33
Kiernan, Thomas, 135
Kinross, Lord, 136
Kittaniya, 42
Kohut, Heinz, 15, 86
Kristallnacht, 116
Kuwait, 49, 133

Lacouture, Jean, 136
La Fontaine, Jean, 37
Laroui, Abdallah, 61
Lawrence, T. E., 9, 141–42
Leachman, Gerard, 142
Lebanon, Lebanese, 80, 124, 134
Lenin, 110
Lewis, Bernard, 13
Libya, 12
Loewenberg, Peter, 108, 142
Longford, Elizabeth, 141
Lunt, James, 134

Mack, John E., 103, 108, 141–42
al-Maghribi, Samuel, 31
Majid bin Khamis, 53–54
Maliki school, 48
Malkum Khan, 128
Malti-Douglas, Fedwa, 130
Mansur bin Ahmad, 42
Mansuri, 'Abd al-Rahman, 42–46, 149n15
Mansuri, Ahmad, 43–44, 56–57, 149n15
Ma'oz, Moshe, 134
marabouts, 42, 46, 56
Marrakesh, 42–43
marriage, 40, 45, 51. See also women
Marsot, Afaf Lutfi Sayyid, 131
Marxism, 5, 92, 98
mashyakha, 26
al-Ma'sul, 42
Mattar, Philip, 134
Mauss, Marcel, 37–38
Mediterranean Historical Review, 122
Mehmed the Conqueror, 131
Mein Kampf, 111
Meinecke, Friedrich, 91
Melman, Yossi, 135
memoirs, see autobiography
Mishaqqa, Mikha'il, 31
Mitchell, Timothy, 140
Mohammad Reza Shah, 15, 69–76, 125, 137, 139, 153n16
Moin, Baqer, 137
Mommsen, Theodor, 93
Monroe, Elizabeth, 142
Monypenny, William Flavelle, 89
More, Thomas, 89
Morocco, Moroccans, 14, 36–37, 40–48, 56–58, 67, 123, 139–40, 150n20
Moses, 22
Mossadegh, Mohammad, 137
Mottahedeh, Roy, 65–67, 139
Mu'allaqa, 24
Mudar, 38
Muhammad, Prophet, 1–4, 5, 38, 40, 43, 94

Muhammad V, sultan of Morocco, 44, 46
al-Muhasibi, Harith, 29
Mukhtar al-Susi, 41–42
Münchhausen, Gerlach von, 118, 120
Munich, 111
Musa bin Haddu, 46
Musa, Salama, 130
Musandam, 49
Musaylima bin Habib, 38
Muscat, 49
Mussolini, Benito, 121
Mütercim Osman, 32

Nacquet, Vidal, 22
Najaf, 50
narcissism, 15–16, 70–72, 74–75, 87, 101–2
Nasir al-Din Shah, 9, 25, 132
Nasser, 9, 121, 136
Nehemiah, Book of, 22
Niederland, William, 99, 106
Nightingale, Florence, 110
Nixon, Richard, 72
Nizwa, 51
Nuri bin Sa'id, 94, 133

Oman, Omanis, 14–15, 36–37, 41, 48–58
Orientalism, Orientalists, 2–6, 7, 14, 38
Ottoman Empire, Ottomans, 9, 20, 25, 27–28, 32–33, 97, 130–32. See also Turkey

Pahlavi, Ashraf, 73
Pahlavi dynasty, see Mohammad Reza Shah; Reza Shah
Palestine, 114–17
Palestine Liberation Organization (PLO), Palestinians, 12, 134–35, 139, 149n14
Pawel, Ernst, 142
Perron, Ernest, 73
Persepolis, 72
Persia, see Iran
Persian Gulf, 49, 69, 72

personality, cult of, 3, 9, 12, 131
Philby, H. St. John, 9, 142
pilgrimage, Muslim, 26, 46
Plato, 91
Plutarch, 89
poetry, poets, 24–26, 39, 42, 51–53, 62
political science, see social sciences
Popper, Karl, 91
Prescott, William Hickling, 93
psychobiography, 10–11, 15–17, 67–68, 74–76, 78–79, 83–84, 95–98, 100, 105, 122, 137, 141–42; and psychoanalysis, 2, 15–16, 65, 85–86, 97–108, 137. See also biography; psychopolitical studies
psychopolitical studies, 15, 60, 68, 75–76, 78–79, 82–88, 153n14

Qajar dynasty, see Nasir al-Din Shah
Qarawiyin mosque-university, 40–41, 46
Qasim, ʿAbd al-Karim, 118, 120–21, 123–25, 133
al-Qays, Imr, 53
Qeshem, 49
Qum, 50
Qurʾan, memorization and study of, 38–40, 44, 50–51, 53–54, 58

Rabiʿa, 38
Rapaport, David, 105
al-Razi, Muhammad ibn Zakariya, 28
Reagan, Ronald, 35, 82
Reich, Bernard, 138
Reinharz, Jehuda, 143
Reis, Sidi Ali, 27
Reubeni, David, 31
Reza Shah, 70, 137
Richard the Lion-hearted, 1
Rida, Rashid, 130
Rifian revolt, republic, 45–46
Rodinson, Maxime, 5
Rome, Romans, 27, 33, 37–38, 93
Roosevelt, Franklin Delano, 71
Rosetta stone, 93
Rouleau, Eric, 139

Rubin, Jeffrey Z., 138
Runyan, William, 78–79, 83
Rushdie, Salman, 3
Russia, 32

Sadat, Anwar, 136, 139
al-Sadr, Musa, 66, 134
Saʿid bin Taymur, 48–49
St. Clair, Barrie, 136
Saladin, 1, 25
Sanskrit, 24
Sanuʿ, Yaʿqub, 129
Sasanids, 23
Satanic Verses, The, 3
Saudi Arabia, Saudi Arabians, 54, 135
Schafer, Roy, 86
Schliemann, Heinrich, 106
Seale, Patrick, 134
self-narrative, see autobiography
Selim III, 131
sexuality, 11, 98–99, 119
Shaʿban, M. A., 94
Shafiʿi school, 49
Shakespear, Captain W. H., 142
Shapira, Anita, 143
al-Shaʿrani, ʿAbd al-Wahhab, 29
Shaw, Stanford, 130
Sheean, Vincent, 135
Shiʿa, 49–50, 66, 134
al-Shidyaq, Ahmad Faris, 31
Shiroye, 23
Simmel, Georg, 65
social sciences, 17–18, 76–78, 83–84, 88, 95–97, 138–40
sociology, 95, 118
Solzhenitsyn, Alexsandr, 110
sources, 7–9, 15, 17, 45, 123–24; archival, 8, 10, 123–25, 128, 129, 131–32, 137; interviews, 9, 16, 47, 105–6, 124, 132, 134; letters, 8, 52, 105, 141–42. See also autobiography
Soviet Union, 69, 81
Spanish (in Morocco), 46–47
Stalin, 71, 121
Strachey, Lytton, 110
Suez, 125

Suhar, 49
Sullivan, Harry, 105
Sunnis, 34, 48–50
al-Susi, Mukhtar, 41–42
Sykes, Henrietta, 119
Syme, Ronald, 93
Syria, Syrians, 9, 10, 12, 25, 31, 116,
    134

al-Tabari, Muhammad ibn Jarir, 21,
    38
Taheri, Amir, 137
Tahmasp, 25
al-Takmila, 125, 139
Tangier, 42
al-Tantawi, ʿAyyad, 32
tarjama, see autobiography
Tehran, 8, 71, 74
Tel Aviv, 97
Temesvár, 32
Tetouan, 47
Teveth, Shabtai, 17–18, 143
Tiglat Pileser, 22
Timur, 25
Transjordan, see Jordan
Tuhami, 66–67, 140–41
Tunisia, 131
Turkey, Turks, 16, 20, 32, 66, 97–
    102, 107, 123, 129, 136–37, 139,
    140. See also Ottoman Empire
twinship, concept of, 71, 73

ulama, 35–36, 41–42, 54–55, 57–58,
    89–90
United States, 6; policy toward Iran,
    69, 71–72, 74, 80–82
Usama ibn Munqidh, 25

Vatikiotis, P. J., 136
Vienna, 27–28, 32
Volkan, Vamik, 16–17, 65–67, 137

Watt, Montgomery, 94
Weintraub, Karl J., 60–61, 63
Weizmann, Chaim, 143
Wilber, Donald N., 137
Wilson, Jeremy, 142
Wilson, Mary C., 134
Winstone, H. V. F., 142
Wittlin, Alma, 131
women, 11, 26, 33, 40, 70, 73, 89,
    95, 98, 119–20, 132, 140. See also
    marriage

al-Yamani, ʿUmara, 25
Yar-Shater, Ehsan, 132
Yemen, 32, 49
Young Turk Revolution, 20
Yusufiya mosque-university, 43

Zionism, Zionists, 110–11, 113–17,
    142–43. See also Israel; Jews
Zirids, 24
Zonis, Marvin, 13–16, 137

Middle East Lives
was composed in 10.5/14
Sabon on a Merganthaler
Linotron 202 by Brevis Press;
printed by sheet-fed offset on 60-pound,
acid-free Glatfelter Natural Smooth, and
Smyth-sewn and bound over binder's boards in
ICG Arrestox by Braun-Brumfield, Inc.;
with dust jackets printed in 2 colors and
laminated by Braun-Brumfield, Inc.;
designed by Kachergis Book Design;
and published by
SYRACUSE UNIVERSITY PRESS
Syracuse, New York 13244-5160

Contemporary Issues in the Middle East

This well-established series continues to focus primarily on twen-tieth-century developments that have current impact and significance throughout the entire region, from North Africa to the borders of Central Asia.

Recent titles in the series include:

The Arab-Israeli Dilemma. 3d ed. Fred J. Khouri

The Communist Movement in Egypt, 1920–1988. Tareq Y. Ismael and Rifaʿat El-Saʿid

Egypt's Other Wars: Epidemics and the Politics of Public Health. Nancy Elizabeth Gallagher

Family in Contemporary Egypt. Andrea B. Rugh

Hydropolitics of the Nile Valley. John Waterbury

Islam and Politics. 3d ed. John Esposito

Law of Desire: Temporary Marriage in Shiʿi Iran. Shahla Haeri

The Middle East from the Iran-Contra Affair to the Intifada. Robert O. Freedman, ed.

The Prison Papers of Bozorg Alavi. Donné Raffat

The Rushdie File. Lisa Appignanesi and Sara Maitland, eds.

The Second Message of Islam. Mahmoud Mohammed Taha; Abdul-lahi Ahmed An-Naʿim, trans.

The Vatican, Islam, and the Middle East. Kail C. Ellis, ed.

Women in Egyptian Public Life. Earl L. Sullivan